Having
Hard
Conversations

Having Hard Conversations

Jennifer Abrams

Foreword by Arthur L. Costa

CORWIN
A SAGE Company

For information:

Corwin
A SAGE Company
2455 Teller Road
Thousand Oaks, California 91320
(800) 233-9936
Fax: (800) 417-2466
www.corwinpress.com

SAGE Ltd.
1 Oliver's Yard
55 City Road
London, EC1Y 1SP
United Kingdom

SAGE India Pvt. Ltd.
B 1/I 1 Mohan Cooperative
    Industrial Area
Mathura Road, New Delhi 110 044
India

SAGE Asia-Pacific Pte. Ltd.
33 Pekin Street #02-01
Far East Square
Singapore 048763

Library of Congress Cataloging-in-Publication Data

Abrams, Jennifer.
Having hard conversations/Jennifer Abrams.
        p. cm.
Includes bibliographical references and index.
ISBN 978-1-4129-6499-9 (cloth)
ISBN 978-1-4129-6500-2 (pbk.)

    1. Communication in education—United States. 2. Interpersonal communication—United States. 3. Teachers—Professional relationships—United States. 4. Educational leadership— United States. I. Title.

LB1033.5.A27 2009
371.102′2—dc22   008038185

09 10 11 12 13   10 9 8 7 6 5 4 3 2 1

Acquisitions Editor:	Dan Alpert
Associate Editor:	Megan Bedell
Production Editor:	Eric Garner
Copy Editor:	Claire Larson
Typesetter:	C&M Digitals (P) Ltd.
Proofreader:	Charlotte Waisner
Indexer:	Terri Corry
Cover Designer:	Lisa Riley

Contents

Foreword

As a child, I can remember my mother telling me, "If you can't say something nice, don't say anything at all." When my older brother teased me, when other kids crowded in line in front of me, when my teachers disciplined me without warrant, I learned to "turn the other cheek," to hold my feelings inside, and to say nothing. I actually felt I was gaining an "inner strength" to withhold my thoughts, my emotions, and my words.

In my early professional life, these behavioral patterns sustained me. Educators are noted for avoiding conflict, for not rocking the boat or ruffling feathers, for holding personal relationships above organizational goals, and for striving to be perceived as "nice guys." While I might be bristling inside because of detecting an inequity in practice or finding an inconsistency between what was being advocated and my personal value system, if I couldn't say something nice, I'd say nothing at all.

Over the years, however, I began to develop a clearer set of values. Through writing, coaching, and consulting, I realized the power of words, that I had something to say and that others would often listen. Do I think, therefore, that I'm now an effective communicator? No, but I'm continually learning, and I'm trying to improve. I wish I had had this book much earlier in my career. If I had only had known then . . .! What I learned through the hard knocks experienced from my well-intentioned but inept, stumbling, often alienating, sometimes disastrous verbal communications could have been accelerated.

In this book, *Having Hard Conversations*, Jennifer Abrams has brought her insights, wealth of experience, relevant examples, and powerful recommendations for taking charge of your language, to realize the power of your communication skills, and to use your language competencies to improve student learning, to create and sustain trust, and to achieve the professional and organizational goals to which we aspire.

From this valuable book, we learn that language and cognition are closely entwined—like either side of a coin, they are inseparable—that words have power, and that through dialogue, we can mediate another person's thought processes by mindfully selecting language with care and intention and thus transform another person's perceptions and behavior. This book helps us better understand differentiation—that language patterns are interpreted differently depending on gender, culture, generation, and style.

I realize now that my mother's early admonitions, while well intentioned, were incomplete. Rather than saying nothing at all, I have learned that there are language tools that I can use that, while they might not be "nice," are neither alienating, divisive, nor conflictive. Rather they are growth-producing, empowering, and educationally sound. I don't have to hold it inside; instead I can choose more powerful language with the intention of helping others build trust, solve problems, enhance self-esteem, and generate curiosity.

Lawrence Peter said, "Speak when you're angry—and you'll make the best speech you'll ever regret." And so we must learn to "observe" ourselves as discrepancies produce internal tensions between what we know or feel and what we experience in relationships with others. As we get better at managing our impulses, we realize that we can have an "internal dialogue" with ourselves about whether this is the best time and place to say something, to consider the consequences, to review the database for supporting our claims, and to have a clear vision of our expectations. We learn that we can assert our values clearly in such a way that others could hardly disagree. We can learn to listen and paraphrase first to more fully understand the other person's perceptions of a situation. We find that empathizing produces bonds of enduring trust and that asking a question is often more engaging and productive than giving answers, making value judgments, or stating authoritative proclamations. We find ways to seek permission before offering advice and to report data rather than giving opinions or making generalizations. In this process we come to realize that, while there are always exceptions, most other people are rational, positively intentioned and only temporarily have they lost access to their own resourcefulness.

Do not expect to become masterful in conducting hard conversations immediately. It takes practice, self-monitoring, self-evaluation, feedback from others, and a commitment to constant improvement. It requires an alertness to situations that demand skillful listening, perceptual flexibility, and careful attention to language selection. This book offers a plethora of examples as well as strategies for self-improvement. It provides samples of language that can be analyzed, studied, and practiced. To begin, you must become aware of the effects of your current language patterns on others. (Sometimes we are not even aware that the language we use may be hurtful, demeaning, or disenfranchising to others.) You must consciously and deliberately plan for using new and more effective language tools and to enjoy the results. You must gather observational data and be open to feedback from others about the effects you are having. And you must make a commitment to a lifelong journey of constantly improving your skills. In time and with practice, these new language patterns can become more spontaneous and intuitive.

Everyone in an organization together would profit from studying, discussing, and practicing the contents of this book. David Perkins (2002) suggests that an organization functions and grows through conversations and the quality of those conversations determines how smart your organization is. Building the communicative competencies of members of a learning organization should be paramount for any leader. How well do we listen to one another? Can we disagree gracefully? Can we take another's point of view? How well do we value each other's style differences? Each faculty meeting, supervisory encounter, parent conference, faculty room chitchat, or problem-solving conversation can provide an opportunity to practice, reflect on, and get smarter at using our language in a professional, compassionate, and positive way.

There is another theme woven throughout the tapestry of thoughts and teachings in this book. Jennifer Abrams is very aware of recent descriptions of effective teaching behaviors and classroom conditions that maximize learning, how neuroscientific research is amplifying our understanding of how humans learn, and of the rapid changes overtaking our world community. She is also keenly aware of our simultaneous complacency with educational policies being thrust upon us by some educators, legislators, and parents who are perceptually bound by outmoded traditions, out-of-date laws, past practices, obsolete policies, political expediency, and antiquated metaphors. They believe that if we can just do more of what we are presently doing—extend the school year, mandate "high stakes" testing, "toughen" teacher certification standards, hold schools more accountable—everything will improve.

What disturbs Jennifer Abrams is that, as educators, we know better. We are aware of the negative consequences of such policies on students' natural curiosity, enthusiasm for learning, and internal motivation. We are sensitive to the effects on teacher morale, creativity, and productiveness. While it may appear that we lack the fortitude and determination to speak up, actually we lack the power of language tools with which to effectively speak up. This book, therefore, is intended to serve as a wake-up call to help initiate change, to validate the enhancement of the intellect as a legitimate goal of education, to invite critical assessment of emerging school practices for their contributions to the development of all children's full potential, and to foster the application of creative thought to designing curriculum and instruction suitable for students today to function effectively throughout the 21st and into the 22nd centuries. Educators as individuals and as a profession cannot simply sit by and say nothing at all. Our children's, our country's, and perhaps our global society's futures are at stake.

"Saying nothing at all" robs individuals and groups of opportunities for continuous dialogue and learning. And as educators, continuous learning is what we are all about.

—Arthur L. Costa, EdD
Granite Bay, California

Preface

Your silence will not protect you . . . for we have been socialized to respect fear more than our own needs for language and definition, and while we wait in silence for that final luxury of fearlessness, the weight of that silence will choke us.

—Audre Lorde (1984, pp. 41–44)

I came into teaching at the age of 22, more than 20 years ago now, with enthusiasm, a big dose of curiosity, lots of boldness, and an exceedingly high standard for myself and for those with whom I worked. I spent the next several years of my life learning what many of us learn—that there were more gray choices in determining how things were done in schools than the black-and-white absolutes I had thought existed.

During this time in my life as a teacher, I learned there were many ways to teach, rather than just one right way. I learned that there were circumstances outside my understanding that needed to be considered, both personal and systemic. Many decisions were made "behind the scenes" to which I was not privy. I learned a bit more about organizational savvy and what that meant, and I learned to be more understanding and therefore, for better or worse, quieter. I listened to the veteran teachers who taught me to play safe and work within the system. Stay small. Don't rock the boat.

Eventually I found that the philosophy of "staying small" wasn't for me. I hungered for a stretch, for some place to challenge me, for some new ideas that would put me on a learning edge. I began to seek out other professionals, go to conferences, and take in new knowledge. I learned that there were better ways to teach than what I saw within me and around me—strategies that were more research-based, more thoughtful, more engaging for students. When I came back and tried to share my new ideas, I found some were welcome, others not.

And I thought to myself, *Why, if we know better, don't we say something? What is stopping us from being our best selves, the best professionals we could be, for each other and for our students? Why are we staying small? The question is one I carry around with me to this day.*

In my first few years as a beginning teacher coach, I took a Cognitive Coaching seminar and had the good fortune of being publicly coached by Bob Garmston. In front of 60 colleagues, I shared a particular dilemma I had been facing. I had been struggling with what to say to a new teacher with whom I was working. She had been, I felt, rather lax in her lesson planning. I was hemming and hawing about how to speak up and tell her I thought she needed to put more effort into designing assignments. Simply whiting out the name of another teacher at the top of the assignment and replacing it with her own name didn't seem to me to be a well-thought-out idea. Had she actually taught what the assignment asked of the students? Had she read through the rubric that was attached and did she agree with it? I struggled with my judgment around this dilemma.

And then Bob asked me a question. "Why do you feel you have to let go of your judgment?" I was stunned. Having been told by fellow staff members that it was inappropriate to criticize colleagues, and that it was so important to keep rapport and not cause bad feelings, didn't we all have to just bite the bullet and be quiet? The coaching conversation that ensued about how one might go about sharing one's point of view in a way that can be heard and keep one's sense of integrity has shaped me and has shaped this book. As the Lorde quote at the beginning of this preface suggests, "[We] have been socialized to respect fear more than our own needs for language and definition." There *is* a way to move past our fears and find the language we need.

I write this book for those of us in the profession who were told they should remain quiet and for those who are quiet by nature, for those who speak up immediately and might get a slap on the wrist, and for those who don't speak up much and then wish they had. Our students are coming through the doors of our classrooms every day, and they deserve our best selves, both personally and professionally. A thousand things are unspoken in schools every day, and the lack of truth telling enforces an ineffective status quo. Change—personal and institutional—requires that we speak *out loud* about what we know and believe. We need to be liberated from those of our beliefs that limit us. We need to find our voice around what matters most.

A SUGGESTION FOR HOW TO READ THIS BOOK

Read this with a hard conversation in mind: a conversation you have yet to have with a colleague that you find hard. Hard is relative. It is something you feel uncomfortable saying and you'd like to find more clarity and courage so you can say whatever you want in the most professional and supportive way. Then work through the book and its exercises with your own upcoming hard conversation as your guide.

With your own hard conversation, ask yourself the following:

What are the circumstances surrounding the concern?

What is bothering you?

What are some of the reasons you have yet to say anything?

Hard conversations aren't ever not "hard." They will always be awkward and uncomfortable, but you can learn tools and the language to make them more professional and more effective. It is my hope that by reading this book you will be more empowered to have those important hard conversations.

Acknowledgments

This book comes from a deep place and a longing to bring emotions and truth into the open and have them received. To those in my life who have welcomed my frustration, my verbal first drafts, my venting, and my linguistic polishing so my voice could be heard, I am forever grateful.

To my parents, Richard and Myrna Abrams, and my brother, Adam, for their love and support.

To my friends, Eric Booth, Jen Wakefield, Greg Matza, John Hebert, John Fredrich, Deb Burgard, Linda Michael, Susan Burns, and Ann Idzik, who all have watched my unfolding as a writer and consultant and were my biggest cheerleaders.

To all my professional colleagues at Palo Alto Unified School District who gave me space and encouragement throughout the development of this book.

To every workshop participant who allowed me to push them out of their comfort zones and who pushed me to hone my craft and share this work with others.

To everyone at Corwin Press who helped bring this book to fruition, especially my editor, Dan Alpert.

And to Art Costa, my mentor and friend, who has encouraged me and supported me to think and grow and learn throughout this process.

I hope this book sparks its readers to push themselves and their institutions to be more authentic and truthful so those within the system can thrive and do the good work we need to do for the students who come through our doors.

PUBLISHER'S ACKNOWLEDGMENTS

Corwin Press gratefully acknowledges the contributions of the following reviewers:

Deborah Ekwo
Instructional Coach
Houston, TX

Susan Chase-Foster
Seventh Grade Language Arts/Social Studies Teacher
Fairhaven Middle School
Bellingham, WA

Becki Cohn-Vargas
Director of Elementary Education
Palo Alto Unified School District
Palo Alto, CA

Janice Ellen Jackson
Professor of Education in Leadership
Harvard University, Graduate School of Education
Cambridge, MA

Laura Linde
Literacy Coach
Hoover Elementary School
North Mankato, MN

Deborah Long
Mentor Coordinator
Merced Union High School District
Merced, CA

Angus MacNeil
Associate Professor of Education in Leadership
University of Houston
Houston, TX

Beth Madison
Principal
George Middle School
Portland, OR

Stephanie Malin
Teacher Leader
Beaverton, OR

Elaine Mayer
Lead New Teacher Coach
Oakland Unified School District
Oakland, CA

Linda Michael
Director of Programs
Region 8 Education Service Center of Northeast Indiana
Columbia City, IN

Ruth Rich
Foreign Language Teacher/Mentor
Rich Central High School
Olympia Fields, IL

Cynthia Rowell
Instructional Lead Teacher and Literacy Coach
Hightower Trail Middle School
Marietta, GA

William Ruff
Assistant Professor of Educational Leadership
Montana State University
Bozeman, MT

Stephanie Strow
Developmental Coach
Fairhaven Middle School
Bellingham, WA

Loren Taylor
Literacy Coach
Columbia, SC

Laurie VanSteenkiste
Staff Development Consultant
Macomb Intermediate School District
Clinton Township, MI

Buck Wall
AP US History Teacher/Social Studies Department Chair
Hillcrest High School
Simpsonville, SC

About the Author

 **Jennifer Abrams** is a professional developer for Palo Alto Unified School District in California and a national and international educational consultant for public and private schools, charter schools, universities, and nonprofits. Jennifer has been a high school English teacher, new teacher coach, and induction program coordinator. She now trains and coaches teachers and administrators on successful teaching practices, new teacher support, supervision and evaluation, generational savvy, having hard conversations, and effective collaboration skills.

She works with cadres of PAUSD teacher leaders to lead sessions on elements of instruction and the "Equity=Excellence" program and provides all new teacher trainings and supervisor trainings at the secondary level. Jennifer also is a lead coach for the Palo Alto–Mountain View/Los Altos Beginning Teacher Support and Assessment Program.

In her consulting work, Jennifer has presented at annual conferences such as National Staff Development Council, Association for Supervision and Curriculum Development, National Council of Teachers of English, and the New Teacher Center at University of California Santa Cruz Annual Symposium. She has trained new teachers in the Stanford Teacher Education Program, administrative candidates at Santa Clara University and international school leaders through the Principals' Center for International School Leadership. Her chapter, "Habits of Mind for the School Savvy Leader" will be featured in Arthur L. Costa and Bena Kallick's upcoming book in their *Habits of Mind* series, *Learning and Leading with Habits of Mind: 16 Essential Characteristics for Success*.

Jennifer considers herself a "voice coach," helping teachers and administrators learn how to best use their voices, whether in a group, in front of a classroom, coaching a colleague, or in a supervisory role. Jennifer holds a master's degree in education from Stanford University and a bachelor's degree in English from Tufts University. She lives in Palo Alto, California. She can be reached at jennifer@jenniferabrams.com.

Our conversations invent us. Through our speech and our silence, we become smaller or larger selves. Through our speech and our silence, we diminish or enhance the other person, and we narrow or expand the possibilities between us. How we use our voice determines the quality of our relationships, who we are in the world, and what the world can be and might become. Clearly, a lot is at stake here.

—Harriet Lerner (2001, p. 239)

What Are Hard Conversations, and Why Should We Have Them?

There are many people who think they want to be matadors, only to find themselves in the ring with two thousand pounds of bull bearing down on them, and then discover that what they really wanted was to wear tight pants and hear the crowd roar.

—Terry Pearce, management consultant

This book came into being when I moved from inside a classroom full-time to outside the classroom full-time. I was delighted with the new role of beginning teacher coach and trainer and took on the job with gusto. I wasn't naïve enough to think I could just "wear tight pants and hear the crowd roar," but I sure wasn't ready for a 2,000-pound bull, either.

In a new setting, with new "students," I had a steep learning curve. And I discovered something important: I had a credential in how to teach English to high school students, but I did not have a credential in how to work effectively and productively with other adults.

This adult learning work was, in many ways, a whole new ball game. I immersed myself in reading professional literature. I took coaching classes and workshops. I learned how to present staff development to adults, work collaboratively to design lesson plans, and move a teacher through a series of reflective questions. Yet one important—and very necessary—skill hadn't been taught to me at all: *how to have a hard conversation.*

Hard conversations come in all forms and degrees. They range from a formal evaluation in which you tell someone he won't be asked to return next fall, to the briefest comment to a colleague about being on time to a meeting. They occur in grade level meetings and in administrators' offices. The content can be about teacher behavior that negatively affects students or about not doing an effective job facilitating a department meeting. Hard conversations can occur when you talk to a colleague about a comment that hurt your feelings or an e-mail you found offensive. Whenever you feel uncomfortable, have second thoughts, or try to avoid saying what you need to say, what you aren't saying *is* your hard conversation.

Teachers come into the business of education to nurture. The best of us joined this profession to be able to work alongside students and support their academic and personal development. For some of us, support looks like praise— all the high fives and "Good job!" comments. Many of us appreciate the feel-good aspects of this form of praise. Support, however, can have a different face.

Many of us can recall a time when someone told us a truth that wasn't particularly pleasant in feeling or tone. Support came in the form of a few comments that asked us to step up, to rewrite, or to do our best work. The truth wasn't easy to swallow, but we knew in our hearts that it was accurate and supported our growth. We weren't doing our best, and we needed a reminder.

> My personal challenge with having a hard conversation is that it is so awkward to tell a colleague who is your peer and whom you work with on an equal level something about her behavior. I would rather avoid dealing with it, but in this case it was a piece of gossip that was being spread, and it was affecting my relationships with others in the school. I couldn't have my reputation damaged. I needed to speak up.
>
> —High school teacher

I was on the receiving end of a difficult piece of feedback just recently. I had been in a meeting where the topic was race and ethnicity. I was so passionate about the topic that I ended up speaking quite a bit. A colleague of mine, another white woman, found a moment to quietly suggest to me that I should be quiet and open the floor up to colleagues of color, who needed to have an opportunity to have their voices heard as well. The truth was hard to swallow, but she was right. I wasn't aware of my own behavior. It wasn't comfortable, but it was a necessary hard conversation.

As teachers, we know we must both support and challenge students to help them grow. We need to also employ a healthy balance of both support and challenge when working with our colleagues.

Many factors come into play as to why we don't like to have hard conversations with our colleagues, but for the most part, teachers just aren't a confrontational group. In our field, unlike banking, which is transactional in nature, we are about more than that. We are about helping people grow up to be good human beings, not just doing a deposit or withdrawal of funds. We are in schools to transform students and help them develop, not just do transactions and call it a day. Relationships are everything in this field. We actively shy away from causing bad feelings. We purposefully did not become litigators, ready to depose others on the spot. We get anxious if a little dander is raised. We worry a lot.

Yet telling the truth to one another, as coaches, as administrators, and as colleagues, is one of the most important ways that we grow personally and professionally.

Think about how often these true-to-life moments occur in schools where someone isn't speaking up.

- A veteran disgruntled colleague gets away with not attending grade-level meetings and as of yet, no one has said a thing. As a result, the teachers at that grade are not consistent in their instruction.
- A new teacher continually doesn't respond to a colleague's phone calls or e-mails. In an attempt to maintain trust and rapport, nothing is said. This new teacher's behavior not only keeps the two staff members from working together, but could extend to her not being responsive in her interactions with students.
- The principal makes fun of a school coach in front of the whole staff, and it begins to discredit the coach's ability to do her job, yet the coach doesn't speak to the principal about his behavior.

Having a hard conversation is a skill for which many of us have no training and little experience. To have hard conversations and do them well, we need some support and some challenge. We need models.

Consider this firsthand account from a high school department chair who had to face the truth to be able to do her job to ensure students' learning:

As the department chair, I have responsibility, along with the administrator, to supervise and evaluate new teachers. One teacher we worked with for two years is a sharp thinker, a kind person, and a team player. The trouble is that she isn't an organized lesson planner, and it is getting in the way of her being able to control the class and teach effectively.

I have tried to be explicit and concrete in my feedback about her management, lesson planning, and instruction, giving very detailed suggestions to her about how she can engage students more effectively by writing on the board a certain way so her back isn't to the students, how clear she needs to be in terms of her directions so she doesn't lose time transitioning, etc. These small, discrete actions, as well as many other explicitly recommended lesson planning techniques, haven't been applied to her teaching.

At the end of the semester, I decided I had to tell her that I would be opening the job up in the spring. The teacher's response was discouragement, and I heard apologies for days. "I know you're right. I'll try. It's just so hard. I am so sorry." All of these comments are excuses you can hear only so many times. She feels bad and I feel bad, but her being upset isn't helping. It is time to find someone to do the job.

This department chair had to get to a place where she knew she needed to speak up, and she ultimately did. Hard conversations are about being true to oneself, doing what is right for students, and shaping an environment that supports learning. We need to learn to do them well.

READY—AIM—FIRE

As I said before, many of us haven't had much support and study on this topic. And while the concept of ready—aim—fire can be a bad metaphor when dealing with people, it vividly describes how, without support, individuals might inappropriately handle having a hard conversation.

Like the department chair above, who at first spent months avoiding the conversation she knew she needed to have, some of us try the "Ready—aim—aim—aim—aim" approach. We just can't muster the courage to say the words directly to the other person. We hem and haw. We talk to our spouse about it, to other colleagues in the parking lot. We complain—a lot. We just don't speak up.

Others of us try the "Ready—FIRE" method. We don't aim. We don't talk the idea through with someone before we speak. We seize the moment, and in doing so, we often cause tears, bad feelings, and unfortunately, sometimes also cause a ripple effect of subtle revolt.

There *is* a better way to have the hard conversation, whatever the conversation needs to be.

GET CLEAR, CRAFT, COMMUNICATE

Let's move past the uncomfortable metaphor of ready—aim—fire toward a new way of framing the work of having a hard conversation. The new approach is based solidly on the three principles of *clarity, crafting,* and *communication.*

Get Clear

- How can we get to a place where we feel ready and comfortable sharing what needs to be said?

This concept will be discussed in Chapters 2 and 3 as we think about why we haven't yet spoken up and what questions we need to ask ourselves before we do.

Craft

- What will we talk about with our colleague? What explicit behaviors are we focusing on? And once we share our thoughts, what next steps do we suggest to fix the problem?

This concept will be discussed in Chapters 4 and 5 as we think about which professional behaviors we are talking about and what our action plans are for supporting our colleagues once we begin communication.

Communicate

- How might we write up our first few talking points or sentences? What language will work for this conversation and what words might just trigger a defensive reaction within the individual and thus stop her or him from listening?

This concept will be discussed in Chapters 6, 7, and 8 as we learn scripting tools for a variety of hard conversations as well as specifics around the *where*s and *when*s of having the conversation.

Mastering these three principles will make the hard work of hard conversations easier. If you've picked up this book, chances are you already know you need to prepare to have a conversation with someone, or you have avoided a conversation in the past that you now know you ought to have.

WHO SHOULD BE READING THIS BOOK

This book will emphasize conversations with teachers no matter your role in relationship to them—colleague, coach, supervisor, or administrator. And while the focus of this book isn't on having hard conversations with parents, students, or support staff, there are many tools in this text that will assist you through those challenging moments as well. My experience has been primarily with teachers, and those are the awkward conversations I know best.

As we move forward, one point about protocols and organizational systems in relation to having hard conversations: In every school or organization there are chains of command and hierarchical systems in place for who is and who isn't to speak about certain topics. In many situations, the policies of your school or district help you to determine what to say and what not to say. Being mindful of those policies is critical both legally and politically.

Yet there are so many times when the choice of having the conversation is one you can make. You are the administrator, supervisor, or mentor, and it is part of your job description to say something. This book will help you have that hard conversation more effectively.

What about talking colleague to colleague? Peer to peer? Both on equal ground? In these situations, things get a little fuzzier, the water murkier. Does that mean one shouldn't speak up? Not necessarily. There are many times when you *are* the right one to have the conversation. You are the facilitator of the professional learning community, you are the grade-level partner, you are the colleague teaching the same course, or you are the colleague next door. Regardless of not having the formal authority, the behaviors exhibited by your colleague affect you and the students you work with. The question or challenge now is to become more skilled at determining the manner in which you'd like to speak. This is where the tools in this book will come in handy.

Hard conversations in schools are essential, not only for our own growth, but for success—our own and that of those around us whom we impact. The issues we don't confront every day—the behaviors we see and the asides we overhear—are visible to us, yet we don't act. We can suffocate under the status quo, and our students will not get the education they deserve because we are not courageous enough to speak up and ask each other how we can be our best selves. To be more authentic and more truthful in schools every day will allow us not only to survive, but to thrive. Yes, the conversation isn't going to be easy, but the fact that it is hard isn't license to not have it.

The goal of this book is to help you have that hard conversation or bring up that uncomfortable concern. The 2,000-pound bull isn't looking that large when you view it from this angle, is it?

SUMMARY

We have discussed to whom this book will be helpful and some of the reasons we as educators at all levels should learn how to have hard conversations with our colleagues. The next chapter will address the reasons why we avoid speaking up, and what wins out when we don't.

2

Why We Hesitate Having Hard Conversations

You cannot plough a field by turning it over in your mind.

—Author unknown

When we think about saying something difficult, people often feel mixed emotions. We know it's important to speak up and to do the right thing, but often those needs conflict with other internal needs. Enid Lee (2002), educational consultant, calls these "the tensions that surface."

Tensions pull us. We have a need for clarity on one side and a wish to not know the details on the other. We have both a need for transparency and the desire to be unaware of what is going on. Tensions are just that. They are the tugs that people face when they deal with an upcoming action, what is drawing them toward it, and what pulls them away. To speak up or not: That is the tension.

Robert Kegan and Lisa Laskow Lahey (2001) termed these tensions "competing commitments" (p. 48). Kegan and Lahey write, "Something else happens if we relate to our fears more actively, by considering that we may not just *have* our fears; we discover we may be actively committed to keeping those things that we are afraid of from happening" (p. 48). While we want to do what is right, we also want to have everything stay OK between us and the other person. We need to do

---

Surface Underlying Tensions

How might "competing commitments" surface, and how can you help that to occur? Ask yourself:

"What is stopping me from having this hard conversation?"

"What am I not admitting to myself about why I don't want to say anything?"

"What comforts do I give up if I say something?"

"What am I afraid of?"

"What is the worst thing that could happen?"

our job, and we would really like just to keep doing what we have always done, thank you very much. Sometimes one commitment outweighs the other, and all will be well. Other times not. When competing commitments surface, we may gain insight into what is keeping us from having a hard conversation. Knowing what is stopping us from speaking may help move us forward.

GET CLEAR, CRAFT, COMMUNICATE: WHERE ARE WE?

Chapters 2 and 3 relate to the clarity stage of our model. This chapter will help you increase your self-awareness regarding why you don't speak up, and Chapter 3 will help you gain some insight into the timing, feasibility, and consequences when you choose to do so.

REASONS FOR AVOIDING HARD CONVERSATIONS

In talking with educators from across the country, they have shared with me their many reasons for avoiding their hard conversations. Some were embarrassed to admit what is stopping them; some were resigned and just admitted the truth.

As you review the reasons below, ask yourself if you recognize any reasons that you feel have stopped you in the past. Are there certain reasons that you believe are your "competing commitments"?

Following every subheading are several quotes from educators explaining their reasons for not speaking, followed by an explanation, a vignette, and then a *Try this*. The *Try this* is there to be an inspirational next step if you have spotted yourself in this area.

Reason 1: A Desire to Please

- *I don't want to look mean.*
- *I want people to like me and to respect me.*

Many educators got into the field of education to nurture others. We enjoy having positive, supportive relationships that foster others' growth. In the face of saying something difficult to a colleague, educators often think that others will consider them mean or unkind. Being liked and respected is an essential need all of us can relate to. Most of us don't want to be argumentative and difficult or to cause upset. Yet for some of us, our need to appear nice overrides our interest in telling the truth to someone.

This middle school teacher faced her own hard conversation this way:

As a woman of my generation, I was taught to be agreeable, to be a connector, to bring people together. So when certain situations with parents arose, there were times that I was less than candid. I would "fluff the pillows" so to speak, and not give voice to my concerns because I was brought up not to speak up. "One shouldn't be harsh," I believed.

One year I had a student who was the only child of two high-powered individuals. This young girl had learning disabilities and a huge chip on her shoulder.

Her mother had a very political bumper sticker on her car, and her father was an abrasive man. It wasn't difficult to see where she got her hostile attitudes.

I cared about this child and couldn't have my fear about not being the nurturing middle school teacher get in the way of supporting her. I ended up meeting with the parents at the end of the school year and said, "You can get angry with me, but you are causing your child obstacles by acting the way you do. You need to work on those behaviors because your child is copying you and it is getting in the way of her being able to succeed."

They could have gotten very angry with me, but they didn't. Instead, they said, "Thank you." I wanted them to like me, and in the end they respected me, and overcoming my fears was worth it.

Try this: Realize the "nice" thing to do *is* to speak up.

Reason 2: Personal Safety

- *I want everything to remain OK—no anger or tears.*
- *I would rather avoid any emotional or physical pain.*
- *I am intimidated. My colleague is very aggressive. It is scary to deal with him.*

Many of us are uncomfortable with others' tears. We don't have the stomach for seeing someone weep or sob in our presence, especially another adult. We are disquieted; we don't know what to say. Others of us dislike yelling and cringe at the idea that someone will raise his or her voice and vent. Loud voices cause us anxiety. We fear we won't be able to hold ourselves steady in the face of those emotions. If someone is threatening you physically, it isn't fair to ask you to sit still and do nothing. Yet being able to hold one's center for the minute or two that someone might cry or start to vent is a productive thing to learn to do.

We may avoid hard conversations out of a fear of the other person's emotional reaction. This is how one sixth-grade teacher handled her own discomfort.

There was a new kid coming into my class. "A handful" was all the assistant principal would say. The child was bright but loud, and he alienated his peers and his teacher by being arrogant and noncompliant. I heard about, and then was the recipient of, his parents' screaming on the phone, and they "screamed" in abusive e-mails. The family was running roughshod all over the school. It was emotionally really uncomfortable for me.

I decided that for the sake of my current students and for the future success of the new child, I needed to set expectations for behavior from both student and parents. I arranged a meeting and calmly set forth what the expectations were. I "personally requested" that there be no disrespectful language from either the parents or the student. I realized that the family was struggling and acting out, so I said, "I am not out to get your son, but we have a reputation of being kind and respectful in my classroom and our interactions will be civil."

It took not getting angry, keeping my self-control, and a few e-mails reminding everyone of the expectations before the anger lessened and discussions amongst all parties were civil, but all communications are far calmer at this point.

Try this: Remember that anything other than civil and respectful dialogue is unacceptable, and focus on that point to remain calm as you express that expectation to others.

- *If I say something, it could reinforce the behavior, and then lots of folks might get hurt.*

You may be concerned that if you confront an individual about his or her behavior, the behavior will escalate and cause even more damage. You are worried the person might respond, "Oh, yeah? Well, I don't care what you think. I'm going to keep yelling at the students no matter what!" Your concern may be legitimate, although that is unlikely. We can consider how to make it more unlikely in a following chapter where we discuss how to frame the situation before having the conversation.

Can you identify with this fourth-year urban high school teacher?

I am very good friends with many of the staff members who, shall we say, aren't seen as "favorites" of the principal. My colleagues are frustrated with the principal because they feel she bullies people, acts incredibly unprofessionally and defensively when talking to adults, rolls her eyes at teachers when she is in the role of facilitator at a meeting, and ignores communication protocols. Several folks have gone out on personal leave; others are made to feel bad so they transfer. I too am frustrated by her behavior, but many of my fellow colleagues have put in many years and are so much closer to retirement. I have to figure out how to speak up on our behalf in the best ways so it won't cause any vindictive behavior on her end. I'd rather be a quiet and supportive ally on the side than make things worse by speaking to the principal and have her possibly retaliate, but it really doesn't sit well with me to be "fake nice." What I choose to do, when I have the courage, is to come to her with suggestions that would help everyone in the school, including her, or come to her with some offers of how to I could help out by working with the staff on something, and then we can do it on our own. I end up really gauging when I share these ideas. Timing is everything. All this stepping on eggshells isn't easy though. I am thinking of leaving in June.

Try this: Ask yourself, "Is there a way that I could tell my truth and manage my communication so that, however defensive the person could become, he or she would be less likely to take out that anger on others?"

- *I need job security, and I don't have it yet. It's better not to speak up.*

In a field where professionals are moving into positions of authority sooner but for shorter durations, many people are just learning the ropes and then moving on. We need to understand that the feeling, "I just got here, I shouldn't overstep my boundaries," both is and is not a legitimate concern. The feeling is understandable, especially for the many new principals and assistant principals. However, the moral need to speak may outweigh the imperative to remain quiet, as shown by this principal in a suburban elementary school, who faced anger from those above and below, ultimately risking her job.

I was a new principal in my community where the former principal was still very involved in the district in a new role. I came in and moved forward with the expected tasks of the principal—observing classes, supervision and evaluation write-ups, etc. I soon discovered that a few tasks I thought were common practice for all principals hadn't been done by the former principal, and my presence in classrooms and expectations was surprising to the staff.

Yet in my gut I knew that I had been given a job, and that job was to make sure that instructional practice was on target and that kids were getting what they needed academically and socially. I questioned my next step. Do I keep my mouth shut, just a few months in a new job at a new district, or do I do what I think is ethical and right for kids and ask for guidance on how to move forward and do the job? I went to the district office, told them my situation. It was awkward and difficult, and there was a bit of embarrassment on their behalf, but I know the type of principal I want to be. I couldn't not do what I felt was in the best interest of kids.

Try this: Ask yourself, "What is the ethical and right thing to do for students?" Judge whether your answer moves you toward or away from speaking up.

Reason 3: Personal Comfort

- *I like it easy emotionally and with work—no waves.*
- *It will take so much effort to do what I need to do if this starts.*

Personal comfort as a reason to avoid difficult conversations may apply to a principal getting ready to retire or move to the next job or a teacher who is just a year or two away from leaving. Those whose underlying tension is personal comfort may reason that even if they manage to have the conversation, the amount of effort that it would take to truly affect change isn't worth the hassle or the fallout. Consider the consequences of staying quiet, as this program coordinator at a high school did.

I am afraid of angry people, and I work with someone who frightens others. She is older, bigger, and more experienced than I am. At times I feel the administration worries about bothering her too. It puts us all in a precarious position, because we need to do our management jobs and there are times when we just decide we won't deal with this person because it would be so much easier emotionally not to.

Unfortunately, a situation came up in a team meeting where one woman made a comment and it offended another colleague. I received an e-mail almost immediately stating that we all needed to meet and discuss this statement with the whole team. I avoided responding for a while. I didn't want to have so many folks at a meeting where anyone might just start yelling. I would need to manage the situation and it seemed overwhelming. I just didn't know how to facilitate that type of discussion, which could have become explosive.

The responsibility sat with me though. It wasn't easier for me internally to deal with the discomfort—I just couldn't avoid my next steps. I went to my offended colleague and asked her if it was OK to have a meeting with just the three of us involved, the comment maker, her, and me. I wanted her to feel safe and comfortable on the team. She ultimately agreed, and the three of us had a really open and wonderful discussion. There were apologies, and then we talked about the issues and our upbringings and how they impact what we say and how we receive comments, and how we choose to deal with conflict so differently. It all worked out for the best.

Try this: Ask yourself, "How valuable to me is my personal comfort compared with the effort I would have to make to result in long-term gains for others?"

Reason 4: Fear of the Unknown

- *I'd rather live with the status quo (even if it makes me sick) than take on the unknown.*

I have spoken to countless teachers who have said to me they would rather take on stomach distress, headaches, pester their spouses with war stories at home, sit in the parking lot and vent, have insomnia, or get colds than deal with the situation or the hard conversation with their colleagues. What you don't know holds greater sway and fear than ailments you know you can manage, as this teacher found:

We worked in an extremely cohesive team within our elementary school. We had worked together for years, we knew each other well, and we'd celebrated and supported one another through many years. When the first one of us left, we were sad to see her go, but celebrated her promotion with her in a huge farewell party.

The teacher hired to replace our friend was nothing like her. She came in with a chip on her shoulder. She was always defensive in meetings and always seemed like she was just biting back negative words. She just seemed angry all the time. None of us wanted to deal with her—and none of us wanted to confront her because we were afraid she'd explode on us, and that wouldn't help anyone.

Finally, as the lead teacher in that grade level, I had to take on the job of talking to her about how her behavior was affecting our grade's ability to work together productively and changing the spirit of collaboration that we saw as the hallmark of our school. I dreaded the meeting, and I spent days being almost physically ill at the idea of confronting her. Yet when I sat down with her one-on-one and began to talk, she broke down and cried. Although she was a fairly experienced teacher and highly recommended, she said she had been afraid to take this job because our staff was known for its family-like ties and she was afraid she wouldn't fit in. She had to see how her behavior had pushed us away, and we had to recognize how our familiarity with one another could be intimidating to a newcomer. Her issues weren't nearly as bad as I'd let myself imagine, and once I understood her fears, I was able to help her fit in better.

Try this: Don't allow yourself to make this conversation more important than it needs to be. Ask yourself: Is it worth summoning up some courage so I can keep my body healthy?

Reason 5: No Sense of Urgency (For You)

- *Not enough kids in the room are affected so let's not make a big deal out of it.*
- *She's been through the workshop, so let's give it time and see if things change. There's no big crisis yet.*

We all have an unspoken threshold of urgency inside. We know when something has crossed the line. We hear it in comments such as, "I'll address this when I have heard it come out of her mouth five times. That'll be my limit." Or "I'll wait until three parents call me with the complaint. Then it will be a pattern of behavior." Sometimes you might feel you need data to decide whether there is really a need for urgent action. Gathering evidence builds a better case, but is waiting for more evidence an excuse for not having the hard conversation? What is your threshold for speaking up? Do you know what pushes you over it?

If a situation is educationally unsound, physically unsafe, or emotionally damaging, even if the action occurs just once, obviously that's cause to speak up. In other situations, "the third time is the charm" attitude may be appropriate, but if you are waiting for that magic number while burning to say something, why wait for a crisis?

This high school department head in a high-performing suburban school realized that students' best interests outweighed his own desire to avoid the conversation.

As department chair, I am the one who signs off on schedule changes for students. Had I been paying attention, I might have been more aware that over the past few semesters students wanted to get out of a certain teacher's classes at the start of the semester. At first it was just a few, and by the next semester there were more, and they were smart kids. They had worked out a system to switch around their whole schedule so it didn't look like "teacher shopping."

I began having a suspicion these transfers were about a specific teacher, but I avoided really looking into it for a while. First, I did not allow transfers on the grounds that classes needed to be balanced. Then I put a freeze on admission to other classes. I postponed investigating if there was something more to it.

This semester, the number of transfer requests shot up and the evidence was undeniable. I couldn't ignore the problem anymore. I needed to talk to this teacher about how she was setting up her classroom community that would cause this wave of students to not want to stay. I hadn't really put all the data together until just recently, and at that point I needed to speak up.

Try this: If you have an inkling of a pattern and similar incidents have happened twice, ask the person for data.

Reason 6: I Don't Fit in Here

- *The culture doesn't address things head on. Why should I?*

Rare is the culture that doesn't promote maintaining the equilibrium. Large organizations such as schools are uneasy with confrontation or disequilibrium and are unlikely to address issues head on. Is that structure reason enough not to try to tell the truth when students' educations are at risk? Consider this teacher's situation:

I began work at a new school, and it soon became clear that this was a school that wasn't "connected" to the school district. If there was a required test to give, some teachers did, some didn't. If there was a district norm to do a certain report, some did and some didn't. If it was mandated that everyone show up for staff development day, some took the mandate seriously and some didn't. I wasn't sure how to work with a staff where the norm was not to do the work the district mandated. As an educator, I actually valued the assessments that were district policy and I enjoyed professional development. In other schools I had worked in it was different—yes, the staff development days were mandated but some tremendous learning came out of those days when my colleagues and I put in some effort. Frankly, it was disappointing to see such a lack of interest in professional development in my new school. I couldn't deal with the disconnect between what I knew was right for kids and the climate I was in, so I went out on thin ice a few times my first few months to say what I thought was important about collaboration and professional development, but the ice was very, very unstable. I was chided for "not understanding the culture" and for not respecting the staff's autonomy and what they chose to do. I don't think I am going to be here very long.

Try this: Ask yourself, "What do I value, and does this school value the same things?" If you do not find a match, you might want to consider a job change. Having identified your own value, find a way to articulate it in a nonthreatening way to others, individually, to determine if anyone else feels similarly. If you find others who do, you may feel more support for speaking up.

Reason 7: Waiting for the Perfect Moment

- *I can't do it until I know more about him or her or that.*

Rapport is a terrific professional asset for a supervisor, a coach, or a colleague. Getting to know your coworkers is essential to collaborating effectively with them, managing them, or supporting their development. The question in the realm of having hard conversations is this: When is there enough in the emotional bank account that one can withdraw to be able to give feedback that might be considered critical? When do you know the person well enough to speak to them candidly? As new teachers come into the profession and possibly leave within two to four years, do we have the luxury of waiting until next year to focus on an instructional weakness that is not serving students? At that point, will we feel we have put in the time so the person trusts us and will respect our opinion? How can we build relational trust sooner than later?

A middle school teacher writes the following:

One of the language arts teachers in my middle school had the reputation among students as being somewhat of a flirt. I had no direct experience of what I was hearing, and I had never observed his teaching or interactions with students since he was in a different department across the building, so I really had nothing to base an opinion on other than what I began hearing from students. I knew most of the girls who were talking were among those in the more "popular" crowd and were prone to exaggerate anyway, so at first, I didn't say anything. He wasn't in my department, and I didn't know him very well. I didn't want to make a big deal out of it or report—what, gossip? I figured it was up to his department head to gather more information if necessary. But I began to worry, both for the students and for this teacher's reputation. I found a time to "bump into" him and have a casual conversation where I mentioned what I was hearing in an almost lighthearted way. I could see what I said made an immediate impression on him. After that, I heard a lot less chatter about him.

Try this: Decide not to over-think. Give yourself a time limit for planning the conversation and a deadline for having it. Don't allow yourself to make the hard conversation more important than it needs to be.

Reason 8: Perfectionism

- *I don't have the right words yet.*

Have you ever been on the phone with a colleague who says, "Hang on a minute; my pen ran out of ink and I want to get down the exact wording on what I should say?" Being very clear about how you say what you say is admirable since words and tone matter tremendously, yet it's hard to formulate a perfect conversation. Waiting for the words to be exactly right could be more about you wanting to get an *A* in hard conversations than about actually serving the other person. We all fumble. Thinking through the trigger words and the specific behavior you want to address is critical. Rehearsing for weeks for the perfect performance is avoidance. Take a lesson from this high school student services coordinator.

Last semester I had a coordinator job with lots of work but little authority, a sick friend, and way too much to do. Although job responsibilities were clear and the work is divided on paper, I ended up doing much more of the work than required. I knew that I was setting a precedent that wasn't healthy, but the reality was I just preferred the job being done versus the hard conversation to get someone to do it.

A new student came to the school, and it was the responsibility of my colleague to handle the transition, have the initial meeting, etc. Her response was that she was too busy. I almost exploded, but I was intimidated by her, didn't know how to marshal my words to say what I needed to say, and so I stewed for a few days while the situation didn't get any better. Finally, I went to a colleague and got help with my words. He suggested such a simple statement. "It appears that you are busy, and I too am busy. And we have to do this, so what should we do? Let's problem solve together." Voila. It worked beautifully. I put out the truth in such a clear, honest form. The words were perfect. I didn't cry, she did the work, and all was fine.

Try this: When you are stuck for words, ask someone to strategize with you. She will be outside the situation and will most likely be able to help you articulate the essence of the request without inserting the emotion you might be feeling.

Reason 9: Distrust of Oneself and Others

- *I don't trust my gut to be right.*
- *I am too judgmental, and maybe this is just another example.*

The distrust factor is a huge impediment for many of us. We have learned to second-guess ourselves. We've been taught by society to discount our instincts, as well as our training and professional judgment. Micromessages, a term coined by Stephen Young (2007), are coming at us all the time, and we subconsciously may put the messages together into what we call "a gut feeling" or a "sixth sense," but we can't articulate exactly is wrong. We may have been told that we are too sensitive, and so we discount our senses and internalize the message that we are overly critical. This is where we need to stop and take a look at the evidence. Is what you are seeing working for the collaborative group, the department, or the class? Consider this story from a teacher in her first year of being a coach:

I was eager to work with the new teachers in my school. Most of those I worked with were in my subject area; however, a few were outside my area of expertise. During the first semester I observed one new teacher in the math and sciences and sensed that something just didn't seem to work in his class. Being a humanities teacher, I felt that I didn't have the "proof" or the years in that type of class to be able to immediately spot the specific problems. Yet I knew on a very foundational level, good teaching is good teaching. I began to realize that I was onto something. The challenges he was facing were truly not subject related, they were student relationship related. There should be a warm, respectful feeling in all classes, even those outside the humanities. I eventually was able to express this to him in a way that he could work with. While his style is still a little more straightforward and direct, he is working with kids in a friendlier manner. I wish I had trusted myself on this one much earlier on in the year.

Try this: Separate yourself mentally and imagine you are standing on a balcony, looking from a distance at what is taking place. You might be right about what is going wrong.

Reason 10: Lack of Authority

- *I don't have enough internal role authority or perspective, and I have NO external role authority. So who am I to bring it up?*

Heifetz, Kania, and Kramer (2004) say, "Prominence, resources, or positions of authority do not define leadership. Significant leadership comes from the margins of society, without authority. What, then, is leadership? It is the activity of mobilizing people to tackle the toughest problems" (p. 24).

I often hear, "Why doesn't the principal do something about it? Why isn't the superintendent handling this?" In many circumstances, they don't even know the problem exists. *You* are in the room. *You* see the problem. *You* are the one to speak up. We must begin to believe ourselves worthy of speaking up. This teacher realized she had the personal power to change things for the better during a presentation at a conference:

I was at a conference when I heard something in one of my sessions that really just clicked for me. The presenter said that what we don't say leads to consequences, just as what we do say does. The absence of words can be as important as speaking them. That really hit me. I began to think about all the things that I hold back on, and what consequences that might have.

I went back to my district and decided I had to speak out about an issue that had been bothering me, but no one was talking about. Everyone was focusing on how high our test scores were and whether we could maintain those levels, but no one had ever said, "What about the achievement gap? What are we doing to address that?" I'd always felt it wasn't my place to say anything, that I didn't know enough about the issue to speak up. But I decided I didn't have to have the answer. Maybe all I needed was the question.

Try this: Read this Marianne Williamson (1992) quote for inspiration: "Our deepest fear is not that we are inadequate. Our deepest fear is that we are powerful beyond measure. It is our light, not our darkness that most frightens us. We ask ourselves, 'Who am I to be brilliant, gorgeous, talented, fabulous?' Actually, who are you not to be? Your playing small does not serve the world. There is nothing enlightened about shrinking so that other people won't feel insecure around you" (p. 190–191).

Reason 11: Distrusting Our Own Judgment

- *It is her choice to do what she wants. Who am I to tell my peer what is best for kids?*

We wouldn't say that if a teacher were physically hurting her students or if we saw someone emotionally abuse a student. We say that when we are unsure of our professional pedagogy—our instructional strategies, such as which reading program to use or how to teach algebraic equations. Yet we do have teaching standards and research-based curriculum. Some methods are better than others, and evidence exists to help you share those thoughts, as this elementary teacher found:

I knew my colleague would get better results with her kids if she would give up her old-fashioned approach to teaching the alphabet sequentially. She started the kids with A and ended with Z over 26 weeks. I'd read about grouping letters for early readers, but I thought it wasn't my business. At my school, we stick to our own classes, and this wasn't even my own grade level. Then I decided, "These are our kids." And how she taught affected how kids learned and what they knew coming into my classroom. I finally showed her the research I had seen. I didn't make a big deal of what I felt were some issues with her kids, but I did point out where I'd found research for myself. To my surprise, she was grateful! I don't think she'd known where to go to find that kind of research, or maybe she hadn't thought about it. Maybe she hadn't had time to look for it.

Try this: If you're feeling unsure of your position, bounce your thoughts off a knowledgeable colleague or do some research to shore up your ideas. Gathering information not only will help you with the conversation, it will validate your own practice.

Reason 12: Fear of Kicking Somebody Who Is Already Down

- *I don't think she'll be able to take it. It will overwhelm her.*

I often hear people comment that it's not the right time to share critical comments with someone because she has just gone through a divorce, or that they don't want to ask someone to pull his or her weight this week because that person has just dealt with a family emergency, or it's not the time to challenge someone to turn things in on time because he just had a major illness. There are moments when we need to be supportive, compassionate, and allow for some leeway. Yet I hear excuses when I hear, "It's just before vacation. Can it wait?" or, "She just broke up with her boyfriend"; "She moved this weekend"; "It's almost the end of the semester, and he has grades due"; "It's almost Friday, and he has looked a little overwhelmed all week." We excuse the adult in this situation although students are not getting what they need. Consider this story from a new assistant principal at a high school.

My colleague and I had been friends and peers for years, so when I took on a job in which I had a touch of external authority over a few of my friends it was really hard to exert it. What if I asked them to do something and they were angry with me? What if they never talked to me again and told my other friends about it? Lots of "what ifs" went through my mind.

In many peer-to-peer situations, they cover for you and you cover for them, but in one case, my relationship with a friend wasn't in balance. My friend/colleague had been going through some personal challenges and even when things evened out for her, she still didn't pull her weight. I typed up a sheet of job responsibilities, which helped immensely in making things far clearer on both ends, but even with the jobs clearly defined, the pattern was set and I realized that some folks might continually be overwhelmed in their personal lives and still need to be held accountable in their professional ones.

I sat my colleague down and told her how hard this conversation was for me. I told her I appreciated her and listed specific things I thought she did well and then went into specific things I needed her to do and the impact it had on me of her not doing them. She cried. I felt like I was adding hurt to someone who was so vulnerable in her life, but she needed to do her job. In the end, she has stepped up and done what I asked. It has gotten much better.

Try this: Ask yourself, "Who are we protecting, the teacher or the students?" And "How can I help this teacher improve so that she feels less rather than more overwhelmed?"

Reason 13: Too Big a Shift in Role Expectations

- *I thought I was here to work on classroom management and the external factors that make up a classroom. Now I am supposed to also focus on something personal and internal?*

Many new teacher coaches or supervisors have a sense of what the job will be like before they take it, but then the actual duties of the job can be somewhat different. Hard conversations come up where they are least expected, as this new department chair discovered:

I was new in my role as a department chair. I was young, and it was my first leadership role. I had a colleague who until we started the school year had been a peer; now she was someone under my watch, so to speak. I began watching her interactions through this new lens and felt that she was having interactions with her male students that might be seen as inappropriate. I went to my principal, who suggested I keep an eye on things. The interactions continued to be flirtatious, and I felt boundaries were being breached. It was awkward because I hadn't expected this to be something about which I was supposed to talk to a colleague. Didn't she know better? In putting the students first, I knew I needed to do something (safety is paramount), but I was unsure of just what was appropriate. I returned to my principal, who left it up to me. I ended up witnessing one more overly friendly exchange in which she offered to work with a student off school grounds, and I felt obligated to ask her if what she was doing wasn't really appropriate. My colleague left that discussion extremely upset with me. I didn't feel that my concerns about the student or about her reputation were heard. Ultimately, another hard conversation took place between the administrator, myself, and my colleague. She changed her behavior, but was extremely uncomfortable around me and eventually changed schools. I know she has continued her career in education and she continues to be well respected.

Try this: Remind yourself of your job responsibilities in your role as coach or department chair or supervisor. Review your job description. Write your own Hippocratic oath for educators and decide whether you are following it.

Reason 14: This Wasn't in the Job Description

- *I thought I hired someone who already knew how to do the job. I didn't expect to deal with these kinds of issues.*

This is a moment of grieving. The job description has changed. We assumed that when we took the job as leader of the team, the new teacher coach, or the assistant principal, that we would be focusing strictly on academic or supposedly professional conversations such as learning theory or systemic change. Now we find ourselves needing to talk about coming to work on time, wearing appropriate clothing, or telling the new colleague not to cry so much in front of the students. We have to deal with hygiene issues, or worse, help someone consider counseling for a drug problem. Venting about how such issues should be beyond the scope of your job and how terrible it all is instead of addressing the matter isn't going to solve the problem. For better or worse, we still need to speak up.

A new principal came to our school and after a month or so, it was clear that many of his interactions were not only unprofessional and demoralizing, but truly emotionally harmful to both students and staff. I held my tongue because I was a teacher and he was the administrator. Who was I to tell him what his job was? He was my boss.

I decided to speak up when I saw a few uncomfortable student interactions, but did so through writing. Unfortunately, he chose not to respond to my letters. At one point, I saw him beginning to hurt the newer teachers, and I realized I had a role to play as a veteran teacher at this school. The new teachers were truly not in a situation to speak up for themselves, but I could. I confronted him at a staff meeting. One comment he made set me off and I said, "Be nice, be honest, or be gone." At that point, it wasn't about our roles and where I was in the hierarchy, it was about treating each other well.

Try this: Ask job-alike peers if they have encountered similar situations and whether they spoke up. Use their reactions as one litmus test. Ask yourself, "Even if I think this issue is beyond my job responsibilities, is it something that is affecting that person's ability to perform his or her job, and, most importantly, is it affecting student learning?"

Reason 15: Too Close to Home

- *This is a small town. She knows my dog's name. My kid plays with her kid. I need to keep this relationship the way it is and not rock the boat.*

In many small towns, or in private, international, or religiously affiliated schools, this tension surfaces often and is a legitimate concern. The idea that you need to live with this individual in your life and in many parts of your life over many years does cause one to ask the question about whether this is a challenge you want to push. What might the ripple effects be? What are the unintended consequences of making this an uncomfortable situation in this realm of your life? Will your children be affected? Your spouse? However, progress needs to be made, problems fixed. So the most professional question to ask in these circumstances may not be how one can avoid rocking the boat, but how to have the conversation in a less "rocky" way and still fulfill one's obligations. This supervisor was stuck in an awkward situation with personal and professional connections interwoven, but she knew she had an obligation to the students:

I supervise a man who is married to one of my friends. I have known my friend forever, know their children, been to their house, etc. So given my personal relationship with the family, it is always very difficult for me to speak to my friend's husband, a colleague, about a professional issue. However, there was a problem and I needed to address it. Parents and students had come to me about students feeling unsafe in the classroom. They were complaining about comments made to students that were too sarcastic, bordering on mean. There had also been political statements being made which were not appropriate. As an administrator, I always ask a parent if they have spoken to a teacher directly, but if they feel uncomfortable, I will speak to the teacher, put it on his or her radar so the issue doesn't go to a point where something might explode. I had the guidance counselor there and I suggested to my colleague that there were pieces of information that he needed to be aware of and perhaps we could brainstorm together what to do in order help him regain some trust in the room. It wasn't easy; I am not sure how I will react for a while when I see my friend, but I feel like I provided some support and assisted both the teacher and the students. You swallow hard in situations like this one, but you move forward.

Try this: Ask yourself how likely it is that your hard conversation will have lasting consequences on your relationship and remind yourself that if you are speaking up on behalf of the students, it will in all likelihood be worth it.

Reason 16: Conflict With Beliefs or Values

- *I don't agree with the program they are asking me to coach, and I just feel awkward.*

This poignant confession is becoming more frequent as educators continue to be affected by changes in education law and policy. As this teacher found out, working in a capacity that goes against one's core values is self-betrayal of the highest order.

I had worked in my school for 10 years when the district decided to convert it to a magnet program. We were all able to stay in our jobs at first if we wanted to, and I did. It was my home. But I had some serious concerns about the program and also about why the district made the school a magnet. I felt like we were siphoning off kids from other school districts that could least afford to lose students, and that the district made some bad financial choices overall in setting up the program it decided on. I didn't agree with any of it, but I tried to follow the program. It was a disaster. I kept coming down with more and more illnesses, until I realized I was trying to do something I just didn't believe in. I really think that inner struggle was making me sick. I eventually left the school and that district and found myself in a much better place. After I left, I wrote a letter to the superintendent telling him some of my concerns. I'm sure it didn't have any effect, but it felt good to get it off my chest. I only wish I'd had the courage to speak up when the administration was setting up the program to start with.

Try this: Evaluate whether a hard conversation will have any effect on your job description. If it might, it may be worth the effort.

Reason 17: Fatigue

- *I just don't have the energy today.*
- *I just cannot fight this battle again.*
- *They already think I am too touchy-feely.*

My colleagues of color often tell me of this tension when we are doing equity work. They have said there are days when they just don't have the energy to fight another battle after confronting inequities day after day. The problems are too pervasive, they say, and they just can't speak up again, or they don't want to be labeled as being overly sensitive. Most of us can think of a situation in which fatigue can cause us to stay quiet, but we try to speak up because we know the consequences are dire if we don't. This teacher trainer did just that: She overcame her fatigue and spoke up.

I had just spent two hours in a meeting with a group of teachers talking about increasing student achievement for students of color. We had been working on this topic with this group for over two days and the energy it takes for me to do this work is tremendous. We had just come back from small groups and one woman said, "Well, I don't think this issue about race is really one that elementary students have to deal with." It was after school, I had had a long day, and I did feel beyond fatigued, but I took a deep breath and in my calmest voice I said, "I don't mean to sound harsh, but I think your statement is incredibly naïve." We went on to talk about experiences many of our children have faced regarding race even in their preschool years. The woman was receptive and chagrined. There are moments when I truly can't figure out how to speak up in a way that won't be too "prickly," but somehow I found a way this time.

Try this: Think to yourself, "I am tired, very tired. But this tired feeling is what students feel in noninclusive classrooms that lack identity safety every day." Know it is worth it, on their behalf, to speak up.

Reason 18: Personality or Intent

- *He is a nice person overall.*
- *She didn't mean it.*

We all work with good people. Educators are some of the kindest professionals around. Yet we make mistakes. Sometimes we want to excuse ourselves from knowing about these mistakes or from fixing them because, "We are nice people overall." If our colleague brings the brownies to the staff picnic, signs the birthday card, always has a good joke on Monday morning, or cheers on the soccer team, shouldn't he be forgiven for being snippy to the front office staff, demeaning to the custodians, or rude to his peers by not showing up at staff meetings? No, he shouldn't. Being a good guy in certain situations doesn't excuse you from being a good guy in others.

We also excuse our colleague by saying on his behalf, "He doesn't mean it." By adding those few words, we discount a person's responsibility for his actions. Intent is different from impact. We each are responsible for how we are perceived. We can't simply say, "Well, I might have said that to her, but she took it wrong and that is her business." We need to be conscious of how our actions affect others and manage our behavior. We need not to make excuses for others, but to help them understand their own impact. Excusing the professionals in a school by saying they have good intentions keeps us from doing our jobs to the best of our abilities. A veteran middle school administrator shares this story:

When someone is told that her contract isn't being renewed, there is often a swell of support from the ranks. There was a teacher who was "non-re-elected" a few years back who was beloved by his colleagues. He was a kind man. Everyone liked him. Yet he wasn't able to meet the needs of his students. When the department comes to someone's rescue, it is so difficult as a supervisor or administrator to remain grounded. Yes, personnel issues are confidential, but it is so challenging to be required to not explain your reasons. Just because someone is a good person doesn't mean that they are well-suited to classroom teaching.

Try this: Try the balcony approach, and separate yourself from personal issues. If you were an outside observer who did not know this person at all, what would you see?

Teachers have shared all these reasons and more with me over the years. They don't speak out due to personal identity issues, interpersonal communication challenges, and out of a survival instinct. Yet there is a cost to us and our schools for not speaking up.

THE TOLL OF AMBIVALENCE

As a supervisor, I often need to find teachers at the last minute if someone goes on leave or resigns in the summer. I know I will do my best to find the best possible person for the job given the constraints of a close deadline, a department that is hard to find a teacher for, etc. There are moments that I know I am not hiring someone who is as topnotch as I'd like them to be. I know that they are serving a purpose in the organization—pinch-hitting for the school—but do I think they are the best educator for those students? Maybe not. But I don't speak up and on certain days I feel very guilty about my silence.

—Human resources director

All of these "competing commitments" and others still unnamed come with a toll. When we don't trust our gut or while we seek short-term comfort, other forces win out. When we don't have the hard conversations we need to, there still are consequences, just not the consequences we may like. Here are four major consequences that can occur when we don't say what we need to say.

• *We feel pain, guilt, anxiety, and loneliness.*

By being silent, we are condoning behavior we don't agree with. While we might be fulfilling our obligations on the job, we might feel that we aren't holding up our end of the bargain in our tacit contract with students or standing up for what we know is in students' best educational interests.

We might also feel lonely. We may feel like we don't fit because we haven't aligned with any one position in a truthful way. In the end, as Parker Palmer (2004) says, "We feel fraudulent, even invisible, because we are not in the world as we really are" (p. 16).

- *We yield control and power to the other person.*

By not speaking out, it might look to an outsider as if we condone the other person's behavior and make it possible for him or her to believe that the behavior is OK.

- *We don't live by our principles.*

Our values are compromised when we choose to let competing commitments get in the way of our need to speak up on behalf of the school and the students. We may feel like a hypocrite. Asa Hilliard, professor of educational psychology says, "It is one thing to learn a method. It is another thing to commit to a philosophy" (Checkley & Kelly, 1999, p. 59). To stand up and speak requires thinking through our position, discovering what is important to us and to others, and committing to a stance. This type of work is difficult for educators, who most often are asked to learn a specific strategy, a new way of teaching cooperatively, or a new set of curriculum standards. Staking out a position requires shifting from learning a skill or content to aligning our identity with our beliefs and our vision of how we should be with one another in schools, a task that requires a great deal of courage.

- *We allow more students to experience a negative impact.*

Ultimately, by not speaking up, more students might have to live with the negative consequences of a teacher's actions. And as Ted and Nancy Sizer (1999) so truthfully titled their book, *The Students Are Watching*.

WHY BOTHER?

Many colleagues say, "We've tried it all. We have spoken up. It hasn't made a difference. No one is listening, and even if they do, they don't back me up." It may be true that many times we don't listen

> I am known as the sweet one in my department, always smiling and upbeat. I never have a bad comment about anyone. It really isn't in my belief system to speak ill of others. But I am beginning to feel less truthful to my beliefs about what good teaching is. It is an uncomfortable feeling.
>
> —High school English teacher

> Year in and year out we watch our colleague continue to roll her eyes, patronize new teachers, and go into these crossed-arm, pouty moments. We just let it go. Some have made peace with it saying that she is like the crazy aunt we all have. And guess what? She continues to be a thorn in our sides at staff meetings and with families. But she does get what she wants.
>
> —Middle school humanities teacher

> There are times when I want to say, "Is that the best you can do?" And I should say it, and I don't.
>
> —First-grade teacher

> I have watched one teacher get away with belittling students for many years now. The administration has tried to put this tenured teacher back on probation but she is one fierce employee. While she fights the district, students are still being subjected to her saying things like "No, that wasn't the answer I was looking for. Anyone else have an idea? Nope, not that one either." After a while I just know those students stop trying. We are doing them a disservice."
>
> —Middle school teacher

to one another. People have their own reasons and tensions for not joining their colleagues and taking action. We don't know what they have gone through, how many times they tried, or the personal toll this "stuckness" has had on them. This idea of resignation is so prevalent and so overwhelming in certain organizations. Motivating and rallying oneself to go against the tide takes tremendous courage and capacity. And yet if we don't try to address it again and again, the problem can't be solved. We need to keep finding ways to bring up what is important, in different venues, to different audiences. Dennis Sparks (2005) says the following:

> Two of the most significant barriers to the realization of human potential—resignation and dependency—are also often invisible to the casual observer. By recognizing and naming them, we begin the process of shifting from resignation to possibility and from dependency to a sense of personal power. (p. ix)

As an educator for the last 20 years, I have struggled with how to shift from resignation to personal power, to find the tools, and to find the courage to speak up again and again so I could be my best self for my colleagues and my students.

A hard conversation isn't the only way I have learned to move teaching practice and our schools forward. By all means, if there is a way to ask questions, try coaching, or use self-reflection with the result that the professionals we work with become better teachers and colleagues, I am all for it. But we need many tools in our tool kit, and when a hard conversation is the most effective way to express our concern for students and our schools, we need to be ready to speak. We need the skills to have that type of conversation with our colleagues. To make a difference in our own departments, in our own teams, in our own schools, we have to speak out in all types of ways that can be heard. And a hard conversation is one way. The tools in the next few chapters are strategies to help us in that specific endeavor.

SUMMARY

This chapter helped us name our "competing commitments," the reasons why we hesitate to speak up and the cost for not doing so. In the next chapter we will begin to consider specific questions around the likelihood of success and the consequences of failure when we do have that hard conversation. In asking ourselves these questions, we will be better prepared when the time comes to speak up.

3

Questions to Ask Yourself Before Having the Hard Conversation

Life is about timing.

—Carl Lewis, Olympic gold medalist

It isn't a good idea to speak up *every* time or in *every* situation that you see something you feel is wrong. Kindergartners shout out answers or have trouble sitting on their part of the rug. From our early days, we are taught to manage our impulsivity, to think before we speak.

How do we continue to develop the capacity to be metacognitive, yet still have these hard conversations? We ask ourselves essential questions about when, where, and why to speak out. It's great to ask yourself, "What makes my own values and beliefs correct and someone else's wrong?" Continue to ask yourself that question, along with others in this chapter, as you consider your own hard conversation.

Questions to ask before speaking fall into different categories, including timing and feasibility, categories that Debra Meyerson (2001) includes in her book, *Tempered Radicals: How People Use Difference to Inspire Change at Work*. Meyerson's categories are used here to sort sets of questions.

Whether you are in the role of colleague, supervisor, or coach, you review all the questions. While some are relational and would be answered differently by people in different roles, the questions focus more on the timing of the conversation or the outcome you are hoping to have and so are appropriate for different situations: principal to teacher, peer to peer, coach to colleague, or supervisor to principal.

By stating our opinions, we aren't attempting just to say what needs to be said, but to have an impact. Before we jump in, we need to consider the "gray space" surrounding the conversation. Read the questions here and see which resonate for you as you consider your next hard conversation. Keep in mind those excuses you tend to use from Chapter 2 so you know your answers here don't allow you to use the same excuse as a crutch but will help you to begin to frame the conversation within these categories.

CATEGORIES OF QUESTIONS TO ASK YOURSELF AT THIS STAGE

Timing

The old adage that "timing is everything" is correct. A well-scripted comment at the wrong moment can be beyond detrimental in having the effect you're after. Consider the timing of your comment in terms of your own frame of mind, as well assessing the emotional state of the other person—both crucial judgments. Consider the following questions:

- Is this a good time to take a risk and pose a challenge?
- Do I have to say anything or will the problem fix itself on its own?
- How intense is this need? Does it need to be handled now, or can it wait?
- Am I in the right frame of mind to say something, or will I become too emotional?
- Is this the time for this person to hear this? Can he hear this now or is his stress level so high my message wouldn't be heard?
- Do I have enough information and accurate information about this situation?
- Do I prioritize this conversation before another one?

Stakes

Thinking past the conversation to the impact on the various parties involved is a critical consideration. The conversation may affect others beyond you and the individual you're speaking to. There may be additional consequences or fallout from the situation. Consider the following questions:

- Who might need to know about the conversation before it takes place?
- What are the worst and best scenarios for what might happen after?
- How high are the stakes for the different parties involved? Is this a discussion worth having?
- If I speak up, who or what else will this affect? What is the ripple effect?
- Are the negative effects greater than the potential gains if I choose to speak out?
- How important is it for students that I bring this up?

- Is what is going on in the classroom unsafe or damaging to students?
- Is this something that the "higher ups" need to know about? Is this a contractual situation? What rights do I have? What rights does she have?
- How vulnerable am I willing to get?
- Is this imperative to talk about or just somewhat important?
- What would happen if I didn't have the conversation?

Likelihood of Success

We all hope that once a conversation takes place things will change for the better. You're in the best position to decide whether a positive outcome is possible. You can better judge the likely outcome with a little forethought. Consider the following questions:

- How promising are the hoped-for results?
- Have I thought through enough what the real problem is so I have articulated it well? Has it come up before? Is it a pattern?
- If I bring up this issue, do I have an action plan? Can I support the teacher through the changes I would like to see made? Do I have a game plan in mind?
- Has this been addressed at another time? If so, how does that information connect to the current situation?
- If I say something, is it going to move the teacher's practice forward?

Options

Sometimes there are other ways to change the situation besides the most obvious one in which you speak to the individual. Other solutions may be more likely to succeed. The person may discover the issue herself, a colleague may be more suited to initiate the conversation, or putting something in writing may be more appropriate. Looking at various options is worth some reflection time. Consider the following questions:

- Is it within my purview to have the conversation, or should I bring the information to someone else?
- Are there better alternative responses that would pose a less significant risk?
- Are there responses that will enable me to take a stand without jeopardizing my credibility?
- Has this person been given the opportunity to discover the issue on her own, and does the person recognize it as an issue? Have I tried to bring it up before, and what was the response? Is there a way I could help the person see the matter as a concern without going into "hard conversation" mode?
- Can this issue be brought up via e-mail or another medium? Which medium would be most effective? Does it need to be said face-to-face?

- How do I feel about offering this criticism? Does it give me pleasure or pain? If I am feeling some satisfaction in bringing this up, is there someone else who can speak out so my attitude won't be detected?
- What am I trying to accomplish? If I speak up, will I move toward or away from that goal?
- What are some other ways of thinking about this issue? Has this always been the case, or have there been times when something different has happened?

Consequences for Failure

Imagining how you will handle potential consequences and repercussions if the conversation does not go well is a useful planning strategy. Playing out a catastrophe isn't the best way to manage many conversations—they simply aren't that critical nor are the circumstances that dire—but sometimes envisioning the worst-case scenario may give you a greater sense of control.

- What are the worst possible outcomes of your different choices? How bad are the outcomes, and how likely are they to occur?
- No matter what the outcome is, is this something I have to say because I have to say it?
- Am I willing to experience the discomfort that might come as a result of bringing up this topic?

Personal Perspective

We all know colleagues who have their soapboxes on which they often stand. Others of us are more sensitive and respond with emotion depending on the topic. Identifying your personal triggers will help you tremendously when having hard conversations. Your awareness will help you separate your personal associations with the situation from your professional obligation to speak up when you see something ethically unsound or professionally inappropriate. Before speaking, ask yourself if the behavior that you are about to comment on is a pet peeve or truly academically ineffective. You will thank yourself. Consider the following questions:

- Will this be seen as only *my* issue? Am I outside the interaction and yet commenting on it heatedly?
- Can I say what I want to say and still project acceptance of this person?
- Do I have a positive, trusting relationship with this person so I can bring up this concern and have it heard?
- Is the teacher doing something that is really a pet peeve of mine or a style difference, or is this something that needs to change because it is affecting students?
- Do I model the behavior I am looking for so after I say something I will know I am already walking my talk?

- Does my silence allow this person to think I agree with his perspective or behavior? Is that OK?
- Am I wearing a cultural lens that I need to acknowledge and deal with?
- How do my beliefs guide me to think this way, and how might other beliefs alter my thinking?
- If I trusted this person's intentions, would I interpret his responses differently?
- Why do I hold on so strongly to this view?

Feasibility

Since your goal is to have your colleague change his or her behavior so students learn more effectively and schools function more smoothly, you have to honestly consider whether the changed behavior you want is actually possible, whether the person has the knowledge and skills to accomplish the goal or can learn. Be clear in your own mind about what the goal you're after will require the person to do in order to accomplish the change. Knowing that is an essential piece in thinking how you might have to help.

- Does a response feel manageable and not overwhelming? Is there a response that I can help implement that would be as helpful?
- Is there specific and reliable evidence I can share? How would I present that evidence in a way that can be heard?
- If I do bring up the concern, is there enough time to really deal with it, or will bringing it up just cause problems?
- Have I thought through why this person might be behaving in this way?
- What external or internal factors are affecting this person? What are her motivations?
- Why would a reasonable, rational, and decent person do what she is doing?
- Is the behavior I am proposing as a substitute possible for this individual to accomplish or learn?

You may be thinking that your answers to these questions have moved you away from having a hard conversation, that by thinking so much about what you have to say, you may never say it. These questions do ask you to reflect and to contemplate whether the conversation is more about you than the other person, whether you have the right evidence to speak at this time, whether you have an action plan if your colleague asks what

I became the special education mentor for my site, and it was my first time working in a mentor role with other adults. When the shock wore off in terms of the work I needed to do—answering requests for materials, watching versus teaching the classes, learning how to give feedback to a new teacher and not hurt her feelings, etc.—I realized I also might need to speak to some veteran teachers about their teaching practices. It is my inclination to just say what I need to say, but questions about timing and likelihood of success really stopped me in my tracks. I needed to slow down and think through the best time to speak up and the best way to say what I wanted.

—High school special education teacher

you can do to help. You may decide not to have the conversation . . . for now. You will be better off having carefully considered all angles at this stage so you can be successful later.

SUMMARY

This chapter has offered much food for thought as you think about having a hard conversation. If you have answered the questions thoughtfully and have determined ways to address critical points, in the next chapter we can discuss what language and professional teaching behaviors we can use to center our discussions.

4

What's the Real Problem? Finding the Professional Language to Name It

Almost all conflict is a result of violated expectations.

—Blaine Lee, quoted in Stephen Covey (2006, p. 192)

In Chapter 3, we prepared for the conversation by asking ourselves hard questions about our own reasons for moving forward. Now that we've gained clarity on why we feel we must have this hard conversation, we need to consider how to speak professionally about our concern. How are we defining what professional obligations this person must yet meet? Which of the job requirements has the person not fulfilled? What hasn't been executed correctly?

We should be able to articulate job expectations and professional teaching behaviors to be as clear as possible about what we expect of a teacher, what criteria we will use, and what benchmarks.

While we may agree a stellar teacher produces magic in the classroom that can seldom be captured in an assessment, we should be able to articulate what being "professional" looks like on a day-to-day level. Schools and districts around the country have tried to put into words clear expectations for every teacher, both veteran and novice. The National Board for Professional Teaching Standards has descriptors of what teaching excellence looks like. California Standards for the Teaching Profession do the same. National organizations focused around specific content areas have them as well. Study after study communicates to us that there is a science to quality teaching.

As instructors, we understand that vagueness gets us in trouble with students, so we offer procedures, rubrics, and self-assessment checklists. With adults, we often believe they should just know better. And frankly, that isn't fair.

GET CLEAR, CRAFT, COMMUNICATE: WHERE ARE WE?

Chapters 4 and 5 relate to the crafting stage. We now should have clarity around our choice to have a hard conversation. At this point, we will begin crafting our talk by finding professional language to use during our conversation. In Chapter 5, we will design an action plan of support. Then we can begin the communication phase and the scripting process.

PROFESSIONAL TEACHING BEHAVIORS

This chapter is placed here intentionally to get us to stop and think about the professional behaviors we expect in our colleagues. Once we have clear in our minds what the hard conversation centers around in professional terms, we can move forward.

Putting expected behaviors into writing and reviewing them may not stop you from having to have a hard conversation, but doing so will help clear up some of the debates as to what is expected and offer common language for those expectations. Having the job description in writing and referring to this existing agreement can make for an easier conversation.

While the outline here focuses on teachers, many of the suggestions can be adapted to other role groups, and if you're not in a supervisory role, your first hard conversation might be to suggest compiling a set of clear expectations for your group. There are many Web sites or organizations to which you can go to find administrative standards, guidance counselor standards, and support personnel job descriptions. Measurable outcomes for anyone in any job are terrifically helpful. Given that the great majorities of staff in our schools are teachers and that the quality of the teacher makes such a huge difference in terms of student achievement, this chapter will focus on teachers and their professional behaviors in the workplace, both inside and outside the classroom.

I have differentiated between the teacher's behaviors in the classroom in terms of creating a safe classroom climate and working with a variety of learning needs and what a teacher's behaviors could be as a colleague and professional at the school. Those behaviors, so critical to making a school work well, are rarely articulated with any specificity. Conversations about gender, race, socioeconomics, and other identity issues are difficult to handle, and while most schools have policies that address these topics, the talks can be awkward. The conversations can become less subjective if the expectations are clear.

CATEGORIES OF TEACHER BEHAVIORS

Although titled a bit differently, the teaching behaviors that follow are organized into six basic categories that are very similar in concept to those used by the California Standards for the Teaching Profession and the National Board for Professional Teaching Standards.

- Classroom management and climate
- Meeting the needs of a variety of learners
- Planning lessons and instructional delivery
- Assessment
- Developing as a professional educator
- Participation in the school community

I wrote these questions after 20 years of work in schools, observing classrooms and studying effective teacher practice. Although these may not directly align with the teaching standards of your state, district, or school, these behaviors are recognized aspects of teaching that are demonstrated by good teachers everywhere and at every level.

These behaviors are not in order of priority. One doesn't learn them chronologically, nor should they be considered to go from easiest to hardest. My choice for starting with classroom climate is because teachers getting ready for the school year must consider how they are going to make their classroom a welcoming and safe place for all students.

After each major descriptor is a brief set of exemplars describing the specific behavior you would see in a classroom where good teaching was practiced. A fuller list of teaching behaviors is included in Resource A.

As you read through the questions, ask yourself, "What else would I expect to see in the classroom?"

As you look through these categories and teacher behaviors ask yourself:

- Within which category do I see the key ideas for my own hard conversation?
- Are there certain words or language used that could help me speak professionally about my concern?
- What specific behaviors would I want to articulate to this individual about what is expected of him or her?
- Am I highlighting behaviors in more than one category? If so, does one category seem most pressing?

Classroom Management and Climate

Classroom management is what makes the class go smoothly—the teacher's processes, procedures, rules, and rituals. If students aren't aware of what is expected of them in terms of how to behave with one another or how to manage their materials, the teacher can't focus on the lesson content.

Classroom climate is the feeling or tone in the class. Has the teacher created a safe environment for students to do their best work? Do they feel they belong in the classroom? Do students work well together and support one another?

How a teacher structures both the management of materials and the tone of the class is critical for effective teaching to occur. Awkward conversations take place when colleagues have to talk to colleagues about creating a safe and structured place for students to learn. See if the list of following behaviors helps you to locate some specifics that will help make your conversation less subjective.

- Does the teacher make clear the procedures needed to have a well-run classroom? If so, how? Do students seem to know what to do
  - when they sit down (bell work),
  - when they hand in a paper,
  - when they move around the room,
  - when they move into groups, and so on.
- Does the teacher have a clear discipline plan? Is it articulated to the students? Is it followed consistently?
- Does the teacher keep track of time? If so, how? Does she verbally announce times for processing activities in order to keep students moving at an appropriate pace? Does she check in to see whether students need more time?
- Does the teacher have equipment and materials organized in logical places? If so, how? Can students get to the garbage can? To the wire baskets? Can they see the notes on the board? Can the teacher get to each student and easily monitor the class?
- Does the teacher move the students around effectively to support the instruction? If so, how? Do students move easily from group to lecture to partner processing?
- How does the teacher attract the class's attention before he starts instruction? Does the teacher have signals for these moments? If so, what are they, and are they effective?
- If a student says something disrespectful or derogatory, how does the teacher deal with that student? Does the teacher comment in a way that makes the class feel safe? If so, how?
- What is on the walls of the room? Are they distracting or over- or under-stimulating? Are the messages positive? Do they engage students?
- How does the teacher redirect students who are off-task? Is redirection done in a respectful manner (i.e., cueing students nonverbally)? If so, how?
- Does the teacher model courteous behavior and good citizenship? If so, how?

Meeting the Needs of a Variety of Learners

Creating a student-focused classroom is not an easy task. The diverse needs of the students require teachers to be mindful of so many behaviors.

Teachers work simultaneously with English learners, students with learning challenges, and students requiring enrichment activities. How does the teacher accommodate and plan for all her students? Being aware of the variety of cultures in a classroom and creating safe spaces for all students to work to their potential is a challenging task, yet we need to do so if our students are to succeed. Hard conversations might take place when these behaviors haven't been seen, and using this language to identify the specifics could be helpful.

- Does the teacher strive to learn about the personalities and social backgrounds of her students? If so, how? Does she talk with counselors, support staff, students themselves, and parents?
- Does the teacher know enough about the students to know which students can relate to certain material based on gender, culture, immigration status, or socioeconomic status? If so, how?
- Does the teacher show an understanding of strategies to support those students who need assistance through special education services? If so, how?
- Does the teacher show an understanding of English language learner (ELL) strategies in order to engage these students effectively? Does she offer additional supports or use specially designed academic instruction in English (SDAIE) strategies? Do ELL students feel engaged and safe in the classroom? If so, what is the teacher doing to help them feel that way?
- Does the teacher know the students and the school cultures well enough to be able to add examples and illustrations that will connect to the students' lives? If so, how?
- Does the teacher pick up on day-to-day "messages" from students? Is he attentive to revealing messages in classroom work or responses? If so, how?
- Does the teacher show respect for all students? If so, how? Does the teacher speak to them courteously, acknowledging their opinions and values, even if they are different from the teacher's opinion?
- Does the teacher use language that validates and respects all home cultures and family structures?
- Does the teacher provide opportunities for *all* students to learn, process, share, and participate, not just those who have their hands up? If so, how? When students participate, does the teacher listen to and look at all students?
- Does the teacher seem to positively presuppose that all kids can learn and achieve? If so, how? Does she speak to students' potential and presuppose they can do the work, or does she speak to their deficits or their inability to accomplish a task?
- Does the teacher understand how physical and emotional development at certain ages impacts student learning? Does he understand the middle schooler, the kindergartener, the senior? If so, how?
- What other teacher behaviors would you like to see that demonstrate the teacher is working to meet the needs of a variety of learners?

Lesson Planning and Instructional Delivery

Traditionally, supervisors or mentors have not had opportunities to see lesson planning in action. Most evaluation protocols use classroom observations as the primary method of assessment, and mentoring is done after school. Looking at a teacher's lesson plans or observing the teacher's participation in grade-level team planning sessions helps the coaches, mentors, and supervisors get a better sense of what questions the teacher asks when he or she designs units, creates connections to state standards, and goes through the critical thinking tasks around choosing instructional strategies. Many hard conversations take place *after* the lesson that could have been prevented with a prior conversation.

Delivery itself has its own set of behaviors. How does the teacher set the lesson and bring out students' prior knowledge, pace the lesson given the complexity of the subject, and offer students a chance for review? Look at the following teacher behaviors to find language to use if you need some for your hard conversation around planning and delivery.

- Does the teacher know the state frameworks and standards? If so, how do you know? Is a copy of the standards in the lesson plan book? Does the teacher write them on the board? Is she using them to plan instruction?
- Does the teacher know the content expectations of the course he is teaching, and does he design lessons that teach to those expectations? If so, how?
- Does the teacher design lessons with adequate amounts of active participation in her class in order to facilitate learning for the students? And when students are processing material, is the teacher monitoring to assess the students' understanding?
- Does the teacher use a variety of strategies to engage students (i.e., video, audio, small group discussion, whole group discussion, manipulatives, photography, games, technology, and other resources)? If so, how?
- Does the teacher urge students to think critically? Does he design lessons that require students to work at the higher levels of Bloom's taxonomy (application, analysis, synthesis, evaluation)? If so, how?
- Is the teacher mindful of the objective at hand? If students get the teacher off topic, does she bring the conversation back to the objective? If not, can the teacher explain why she decided not to do so?
- Does the teacher use an anticipatory set to bring forward students' prior knowledge and connect them to the current learning?
- Is the teacher aware of how long a given activity will take, and does he adjust the lesson based on the group's level of understanding?
- Does the teacher model for the students whatever process or format students will need to use (show sample papers, go through an example of an assignment, demonstrate the lab before the students are required to do it independently)? If so, how?

- When the teacher provides instruction, do you hear her using specific examples? If so, how? Do the teacher's reference connections seem to make sense to the students?
- Does the teacher make accommodations so students have options or can change the conditions in a given assignment? If so, how?

Assessment

Summative assessments are normally done away from the eyes of colleagues or supervisors. With professional learning communities more active in schools and the collection of student data becoming more of a common practice, colleagues are seeing all types of assessments. What types of assessments are taking place? Is the teacher's assessment *for* learning or *of* learning? Are teachers assessing for the students' sakes, so they can learn even more to increase their understanding, or is it a type of performance or test teachers are looking at to see a final product? What does the teacher do with the information? What is being assessed: effort or content? How many assessments is the teacher doing, and what shows up in the student's grade? And how are teachers working with state tests? What is their attitude toward those types of tests, and what support are they giving students in order to be successful?

Many hard conversations take place after parents' complaints about a teacher's grade determinations. Tense meetings happen when teachers are asked to calibrate their grading with others. This short set of questions does not begin to express the sophistication involved in assessing students. Here are some basic questions that can, however, get the ball rolling in terms of expected behaviors around which you might have a hard conversation:

- Do you see the teacher walking around the room to check on students' progress? Does the teacher check on all students?
- Is the teacher able to gauge students' progress and, if asked, do a quick analysis of how a student is doing in class, possibly without looking at the grade book?
- Does the teacher have rubrics, clear assignment sheets, and clear directions? Are the assignments posted, as well as offered to the students?
- Does he share updates on grades and current progress so students are aware of how they are doing? If so, how?
- Does the teacher have in place a self-assessment system that helps students identify learning goals and use the information to improve their achievement?
- Does the teacher have an evaluation system that allows for feedback regarding effort and not just academic competency?
- Does the teacher use a wide variety of appropriate assessments? Does the grade book include more than one type of grade, including a mix of projects, journals, tests, and essays?

Developing as a Professional Educator

One category of teacher behavior less discussed than others is the teacher's development as a professional. Professionalism encompasses a teacher wanting to grow professionally, honing his or her practice, and taking charge of his or her learning. You can see these behaviors outside the classroom in reflective conversations, staff meetings, or team collaboration. Hard conversations often take place around issues of consciousness, a willingness and capacity to be reflective, and a teacher's interest to improve his or her practice. This language might be helpful as you begin to craft the conversation.

- Does the teacher attend workshops, afternoon sessions, weekend retreats, staff development days, and collaborative/grade-level planning sessions? If so, which ones, and why?
- Does the teacher apply knowledge gained from these experiences into her teaching? If so, how? Do you see evidence of school- or districtwide initiative content or skills applied in her teaching?
- Does the teacher have a sense of what he wants to learn, and does he take proactive steps to have that learning take place? Does he ask for professional development funds, plan to observe peers, and ask for a substitute to allow for professional learning time?
- Does the teacher consistently reflect on and analyze her teaching?
- When she reflects on a class, does she then adjust her practice as a result? If so, how? Can she see what the "take-aways" are? What might the teacher change for the next class session, given the learning?
- When the teacher reflects on his instruction, does the tone of the dialogue seem to blame kids and their abilities ("They can't do it"), or is the tone less defensive and more self-aware ("I don't think I was clear enough with them here and here")?
- Does the teacher seek others' perspectives and innovative ideas? If so, how? Do you hear the teacher say, "What do you think of . . . ?" or "Do you have an idea for . . . ?"
- When offered a suggestion for change, does the teacher use a "Yeah, but . . ." response or does she think about the suggestion and its application in the classroom?
- Does the teacher continually refine lessons and units, and work to improve his teaching? If so, how?
- If the teacher is given feedback, does she listen to it and react appropriately, changing behavior if necessary? If so, how?

Participation in the School Community

Bryk and Schneider (2002) have said that the way for schools to improve and support students in increasing achievement is for teachers to work well together. Professional learning communities, small schools, and learning teams all are designed for teachers to work together to help students succeed.

Most educators are used to spending the majority of our time with children and teenagers. With all that schools are doing with key initiatives such as lesson study or curriculum mapping, schools need a different kind of specificity with regard to what it means to collaborate. Being as clear as possible about collaborative behaviors is becoming critical. Hard conversations happen around these collaborative behaviors we seem to expect from teachers yet expect without proper training or well-articulated expectations. Institutions need to be clear about the following types of behaviors.

- Does the teacher show up on time or late?
- Is he present at staff meetings, at department meetings, on staff development days, at team meetings, and at events related to school improvement?
- Is the teacher aware of the school's values and norms, the way the school sees itself? Does the teacher work well within those values? If so, how? Does she embody them or just give them lip service?
- Does the teacher show consideration for others' feelings? Does he say, "Hello," "Thank you," "I'm sorry," and "What can I do to help?"
- Does the teacher gossip or speak poorly of colleagues in your presence or to students?
- Does the teacher cooperate with special education staff and counselors so that services are provided to the students? Does she fill out the progress reports and make the required or suggested accommodations with a positive attitude?
- Does the teacher manage his anxiety in an appropriate way, not by yelling at staff or students?
- Does the teacher know the hierarchy of positions in the school? Does she go to the appropriate person for the appropriate concern? Does the teacher seek out help to form solutions instead of just existing with the problem?
- Does the teacher want to work in a group and show that through body language, contributions, and attitude? Does he seek to understand the other person's point of view?
- Does the teacher allow for others to participate equitably during meetings, or does she find it difficult not to interrupt to insert her point of view?

EDUCATION ETIQUETTE

In one school in which I work, staff turnover has been tremendous in the last three years. As new teachers came to the school, veterans noticed a lack of understanding of what they see as professional behavior. The newcomers weren't signing up for adjunct duty, certain new teachers were arriving at school just before the bell rang, and some wore clothes that they wore as students. Others looked at their watches during staff meetings or simply left early, saying they needed to pick up their children from day care. They weren't sending RSVPs and sometimes stopped going to the lunchroom so they could finish up work and leave 15 minutes after the students. Veteran teachers were frustrated that the norms of "professionalism" weren't being followed, and the new teachers weren't catching on that there was an unspoken code of conduct.

This school and many others now have realized that they need to put in writing some of the behavioral expectations that had been taken for granted in the past. Many of the communication snafus or the awkward challenges adults deal with in schools are simply not put into the teaching standards of the school and perhaps need to be articulated. Some more recent challenges educators face are the following:

- Can I really collaborate with this colleague if he is text messaging during our meeting and I find it distracting and disrespectful?
- How awkward will it be when I have to tell my colleague that parents are complaining about her skirts being too short and tight? While she could argue that it's the style these days, it is impacting her ability to communicate with parents.
- What will we do about the e-mail discussions going on among staff that include too many "reply alls"? Some of what is being said needs to be discussed face-to-face.
- How do we deal with those teachers who are not being collegial about room sharing? With all these new teachers joining us, do we need a protocol for how to share room space?

Bryk and Schneider (2002), who were working at the time with the University of Chicago, studied the concept of "relational trust" in schools and how trust affects student achievement. While it may be hyperbole to suggest that repeatedly not saying hello to your colleague in the hallway compromises students' academic growth, the statement is in many ways accurate. Courtesy, personal regard for one another, respect for one another's competence, and belief in our colleagues' intentions to support students all factor into our ability to work effectively as a team. How we greet each other in the hallway is just the beginning.

This list of "school savvy etiquette" was compiled from educators' complaints from across the country. It encompasses aspects of school life that can be irksome but for which we seldom see explicit expectations. These aren't the biggest challenges schools are facing, but these little things can add up to unspoken frustrations between coworkers.

Spell out your own school's norms in writing. Use the following list of some school savvy behaviors as a starting point. There is an extended list of school savvy behaviors in Resource B at the back of the book.

- Are there certain protocols for how to send e-mails? Is there an understanding of what content should or should not go into an e-mail?
- Do you have norms for your staff or department meetings?

- Does the staff know whom to go to and whom not to go to for office support?
- Is there an implicit or explicit dress code for teachers? Is there a student dress code that teachers should also follow?
- Has anything been put in writing about sharing classroom space? Are there agreements about materials or cleanliness?

THE CRAFT OF TEACHING

Some may consider all of these behaviors as just "good" teaching behaviors and the bottom line in terms of expectations. You might consider most of this chapter a description of the "science" of teaching.

Some educators are interested in making sure management is smooth, and if things are quiet, all is well. Others worry about students' emotional safety and watch teachers for innuendo, sarcasm, and tone. Some supervisors or mentors care about how well teachers work together in their departments, while others don't emphasize collaboration at all. Some want to see whether teachers have the standard for the lesson written on the board and whether teachers adhere to the pacing guide, while others worry if they don't hear students' laughter and lots of talk in the classroom. Depending on where you live, the grade level or subject you are working with, and your school's goals and culture, you will have a different perspective on the craft of teaching. You will emphasize certain behaviors over others. Being clear with your colleagues about what is essential and what is valued is the key.

> **How to use the list of teacher behaviors**
>
> - Put them in a school handbook if the staff turnover is high and the handbook is used frequently.
> - Attach the list to evaluation paperwork before the write-up is due.
> - Create a self-assessment checklist that teachers review for a professional development plan, during an evaluation, etc. Have teachers note which behaviors they do well and supporting evidence, along with checking off a behavior or two to work on during the school year. One district's evaluator asks teachers to "toot your horn" before any observation, describing in advance what behavior the evaluator will see and giving the teacher a change to reflect.
> - Give the lists to new or veteran teacher coaches to use as teaching tools during coaching sessions or trainings, modifying the language to, "Do I . . ." Lists make it easier for coaches or mentors to develop action plans with their new teachers.

SUMMARY

We leave this chapter better equipped with professional language, having articulated a set of expectations. You might feel ready to address your challenge and move straight into writing a script. But there is a crucial step first—the outcome map.

The next chapter introduces you to the outcome map, an action planning map that will help you support your colleague once the hard conversation takes place. It is the lynchpin for all remaining work that will get us to your hard conversation.

5

Making a Plan

Go slow to go fast.

—Anonymous

A new department chair was told to talk to a teacher who allegedly was not following the assigned curriculum. The principal told her that it was now her job to "Just take care of it." This department chair was the kind of person who would rather just get unpleasant tasks over with, so she found the teacher during the teacher's prep period and gave him the news. She told the teacher to get with the program.

He was upset. He'd been having a hard time with a new set of text-books. After floundering, he said he'd just done what he thought was right. The more frustrated he got, the more riled he became. He lashed out at the department chair, asking a series of difficult questions: "What exactly are your expectations?" "What support have you given me in making the transition?" "What support will I get now, at this point in the year?"

The department chair was taken aback at the teacher's emotional response, but even more embarrassed that she didn't have anything specific to offer about what she wanted the teacher to do next or what resources she had to offer him. She realized she'd begun this conversation prematurely.

Before beginning a hard conversation, you must be able to articulate the professional behavior that is lacking and be able to explain the gap between what someone was asked to do professionally and what is currently happening.

Having looked at teacher behaviors in the previous chapter and articulated your concerns in language that is professional, your next step is to identify how to help the person make the change you want to see. An *outcome map* is a tool to help us do two key things: one, articulate even more distinctly the steps to reaching the desired outcome, and two, figure out how we can support the person once the hard conversation has taken place.

Why not just start in with a script? Why do this map first? *Before* scripting your conversation, working through an outcome map will help you to identify what you would like to see the person do differently, to understand what obstacles may be preventing the person from behaving in a way that you believe would better benefit students and colleagues, and to think about the supports you can offer.

In plain language, when the person says to you, "What do you want me to do about it?" or "What supports can you help me with?" you'll have an answer if you have done an outcome map.

THE OUTCOME MAP

Unlike a roadmap that directs you to go south on the interstate or left at a particular corner, the outcome map (Garmston & Wellman, 1999) will help you to navigate the more complex landscape of effecting change. It is a map in the sense that if you take the time to work through it, you will have a better chance of reaching your "destination" (i.e., the desired change). Although the map appears brief and straightforward, you will undoubtedly need more than a few minutes to complete it—especially the first time—but it is well worth it. Remember the quote: "Go slow to go fast." By thoroughly developing your outcome map, you will set the stage for supporting change.

Some readers might initially balk at the idea of something so structured. It may even strike you as cumbersome or even overwhelming. I encourage you to ease into the process by answering each question with at least one or two bullets points to start.

Use the figures at the end of this chapter as graphic organizers to answer the questions. Samples of outcome maps that have been filled in also will help you understand how to plan your own.

Question 1: What Is the Presenting Problem?

This question asks you to clearly frame the issue. What is your "thesis statement"? What, in six words or less, is the challenge? Is the subject of your conversation poor classroom management? Does this teacher not collaborate in faculty meetings? Is he having difficulty working with English language learners? State the problem succinctly. This step is called "defining the presenting problem." Identifying one key challenging behavior is the logical place to begin. As you move forward in the mapping process, you may be able to identify other factors as the root causes of the problem. At that point, you can revise your whole map. For now, simply present the most precise, succinct description of the problem and use language from the last chapter to help you do it in a professional manner.

> Paraphrase the problem and get it into a clear, concise statement.

Examples of Presenting Problems

- *Supervisor to principal*
  The principal is not performing her supervisory role.
- *Principal to teacher*
  The teacher is not working well with a struggling student.
- *Coach to teacher*
  The teacher is not designing lessons that get all students actively participating.
- *Peer to peer*
  My colleague isn't participating in collaborative meetings consistently or taking responsibility for the work we need to do.

Question 2: What Is the Tentative Outcome?

Once the problem is defined, move on to your desired outcome. At this point, your outcome will be "tentative." By using the word "tentative," we give ourselves permission to try an outcome to see whether it is the right one. An outcome is simply what you would see if the problem were eliminated. We need to move from where we are to where we want to be.

> Articulate the solution concretely. What would you like to see happening instead of what is occurring now? What is your ideal outcome?

Some people find it exciting to sit in the drama of a problem, to stew and vent, but it isn't nearly as helpful as *moving toward* what the situation would look like *if it were resolved*. Instead of a noisy, disorganized classroom, do you want to see a well-paced, well-managed class? Are you hoping that instead of a difficult, argumentative mindset in team meetings, you'll see more collaborative behaviors? Instead of seeing a teacher use only lecture as a strategy, are you looking for a more varied use of instructional strategies that engage all learners? All of these are existing situations that include movement toward the desired outcome.

To first state the problem (ineffective classroom management) and then state the opposite (class should have a well-paced, well-transitioned flow) is a necessary step toward successfully resolving the problem. Speak of what you want, not what you don't.

Examples of Tentative Outcomes

- *Supervisor to principal*
  The principal will do her job as supervisor.
- *Principal to teacher*
  The teacher will accommodate, as best as she can, this specific student's needs.
- *Coach to teacher*
  The teacher will alter his lesson plans and his instruction by including active participation.
- *Peer to peer*
  My colleague will come to department meetings and take on responsibilities given to her.

Question 3: What Are the Desired Behaviors You'd Like to See and Hear?

This is the part of the process where specificity and precision mean everything. This is where we get clear—and move from broad, imprecise goals (e.g., "better communication with colleagues" or "more effective classroom management") and begin to strategically focus on what these things will *look like* or *sound like*. For example, what *actions* could a teacher take that would provide evidence that he was managing a group more effectively? What would his students be doing? What behaviors would your colleague demonstrate to show you she was interested in becoming a better communicator?

> What specific and measurable things would you like to see or hear when the problem is solved? Keep your statement focused on behaviors one can see, hear, and repeat.

At this point, try to think of at least four to five specific desired behaviors in this part of the map and ask yourself, "Am I being concrete enough?" "Will he understand what is expected of him?" "Will she know what needs to be corrected?" For example, "No sighing or rolling your eyes" is much clearer than "be more respectful of your colleagues."

Examples of Desired Behaviors

- *Supervisor to principal*
  The principal will
  - complete evaluations for each teacher due for evaluation this year,
  - complete the evaluations on time,
  - schedule all department meetings at the beginning of the year,
  - attend departmental planning meetings at least three times a year, and
  - report to the supervisor when a teacher isn't following his or her job description and plan out next steps with the teacher.

- *Principal to teacher*
  The teacher will
  - review the individualized education plan (IEP) for suggested accommodations and put accommodations into practice,
  - talk to parents about how homework is done in their house and ways the parents can help the student,
  - check in with the student at least twice during the period and make sure he is on track and understands the material,
  - meet with the student once a week during a prep period or after school to either review or preview material or to explain or reexplain the assignment to the student, and
  - communicate with the family weekly about what is going on in class and write down specific requests for the parents to help with homework.

- *Coach to teacher*
  The teacher will
  - create lesson plans with student activities or checks for understanding that will take place at least every 10 minutes during the hour,
  - monitor students' work by walking around the room during this time to make sure all students are engaged,
  - determine when think time is appropriate before a given activity and manage that wait time so all students have a chance to think, and
  - offer students a variety of activities during these active engagement moments.

- *Peer to peer*
  I'd like my colleague to
  - attend both planned meetings each month,
  - come to the meeting on time with all responsibilities for that meeting completed prior to her arrival,
  - let colleagues know at least an hour ahead of the meeting if she cannot attend and schedule a time with the colleagues to review what happened during the meeting, and
  - take on a number of responsibilities equal to those of her grade-level partners.

Question 4: What Knowledge, Skills, and Dispositions/Attitudes Does This Person Need to Act According to the Desired Outcome?

In addressing this question, we must begin to examine this person's "internal resources." What knowledge, skills, or dispositions does this person have at his or her disposal? What do you think he or she needs at this time in order to do the behaviors? At this point, try to become flexible in your thinking. Try to "inhabit the mindset" of your colleague and understand what internal obstacles might keep him or her from achieving the desired goal. In many cases, the problem may be a lack of skill, knowledge, or emotional awareness. Which internal resources, if developed, will help your colleague move forward?

> What knowledge, skills, or awareness (internal resources) would the person need in order to act as desired?

Consider these questions:

- When one thinks about this challenge, does it require knowledge? Critical thinking skills? Emotional maturity? All three?
- Is there information or are there tools that the person doesn't have?
- Is your colleague confused about his role (e.g., does he think he needs to be the tough guy or content deliverer, when what is really needed is to play more of a nurturing role)?

- Is there a social force or influence that needs to be acknowledged, worked with, or removed? Is the person influenced strongly by another colleague, often consulting with the union representative, or eating lunch each day with another teacher? Is someone stopping the change by saying it is "uncool" to do what is required?
- What can be done to enforce action, or to value, acknowledge, clarify, or give permission to the person to move forward? For example, would a written set of instructions or a diagram lead to greater understanding? Or if one was actually told it was "OK" or "given permission" to use some of the class time to ask about the students' weekend, would that help the teacher to change his practice?
- Are your colleague's beliefs somehow in conflict with what you believe is the most appropriate course of action?

Consider and record the internal obstacles (e.g., knowledge, skills, dispositions, or belief systems) that may prevent your colleague from achieving the desired behavior. Write what you think might stop this person from making the change and what you think he or she needs in terms of knowledge, skills, or attitude.

Examples of Needed Knowledge, Skills, Behaviors

- *Supervisor to principal*
  The principal needs
  - to be given a clearly outlined list of expectations for the job as supervisor,
  - to be given a calendar of her deadlines for supervision put in writing and discussed with her verbally,
  - to be reminded that she needs to take on the role of principal and not remain at a peer level with her colleagues,
  - to be provided support as she "becomes" the supervisor—a colleague to lean on to whom she can vent and who can be a cheerleader, and
  - to be reminded that her role as boss means those she supervises will not always treat her as a friend.

- *Principal to teacher*
  The teacher needs
  - to be provided with the IEP, copied for her in its entirety,
  - to gain or learn additional skills to be able to accommodate this student's specific needs,
  - to create lesson plans in which there is plenty of time to check for understanding,
  - to take ownership of this challenge, and
  - to believe that ownership is manageable and that she has the necessary skills.

- *Coach to teacher*
  The teacher needs

○ to be provided with strong support in lesson planning,

○ to be provided with a tool kit of active participation strategies that make sense for his subject area,

○ to understand that his role isn't just as content deliverer but also as a facilitator of student learning,

○ to rethink the amount of content or which content to include in a lesson if he is now including a significant number of minutes of processing,

○ to create a room setup that allows the teacher and the students to engage with each other in the content,

○ to feel comfortable with a level of noise in his room,

○ to be able to give students clear directions for the activity, and

○ to be able to bring students back from the activity to a whole group discussion/review.

- *Peer to peer*
  I'd like my colleague

  ○ to be aware of her impact on others when she doesn't come to the meeting;

  ○ to understand her impact on others when she doesn't contribute her fair share to the design of lessons or assessments;

  ○ to believe that part of her job is that of collaborative colleague, not just classroom teacher; and

  ○ to believe that she too will get something out of attending the meeting.

Question 5: What Strategies Can You Use to Promote This Person's Growth?

Now that you've analyzed the desired outcomes and behaviors and considered the internal resources the person needs in order to change, you can focus on ways to help the person actually implement the change. Consider the following examples:

- Would additional training give him or her needed knowledge?
- Will watching a video of the class lead to greater self-awareness and, ultimately, better teaching?
- Would coaching help this teacher more effectively plan lessons?
- Would gentle but clear reminders before department meetings, as well as feedback after meetings, lead to improved collaboration?

> What specific strategies could you use to address this person's needs? Given what you know about the person, what language or actions might help him or her behave as desired?

In sum, what strategies can you think of that would help the person actually reach the desired state and outcome you'd like to see? As you formulate strategies, consider some of the reasons Michael Fullan (1990) suggests why people resist change:

They don't know what to do (lack of knowledge).

They don't know how to do it (lack of skills).

They don't know why they are doing it (lack of purpose).

They feel the workload and pressure are too much (fast pace).

They don't feel they will have help (lack of support).

They are worried about failing (fear about performance/self-image).

Many people are tempted to jump to a solution without appropriate reflection, just like close friends with whom you share a problem and who quickly offer you a suggestion to fix it. The list of behaviors you formulated up to this point will help you arrive at the best possible strategy. By carefully considering your desired outcomes and thoughtfully looking at the internal resources needed to help a person to change, you can develop effective strategies to reach your desired outcome.

Examples of Strategies

- *Supervisor to principal*
  - Provide a list of job expectations.
  - Offer a written calendar of her deadlines and set up a time to discuss this calendar with her face-to-face.
  - Acknowledge how her changed role from peer to supervisor has changed her relationship with teachers.
  - Set up regular meetings to mentor her about ways to ease the awkwardness of conversations with her former peers.
  - Share experiences in which you too felt you were the target of unfavorable emotions as the new boss.

- *Principal to teacher*
  - Make sure to meet to review the expected accommodations.
  - Provide time and assistance from the special education department or a coach so the teacher can develop or review the skills needed to accommodate this student's particular needs.
  - Be explicit about the need for lessons that include time to check for understanding.
  - Observe and have a coach observe for other accommodations that could easily be implemented and offer praise for those that have been.
  - Be explicit that she needs to take ownership of the challenge, and help her see she has the skills to do the job.
  - Offer additional support in terms of her tasks, but be clear that the support will not be pullouts.

- *Coach to teacher*
  - Check to see whether the teacher has taken a lesson planning and pedagogy course so he understands the vocabulary you are using.

o Review the concept of active participation.

o Provide a tool kit of strategies.

o Model strategies within his class or go with him to another class in his subject area to see how they are implemented.

o Acknowledge that he is comfortable in a role that makes him feel efficacious and effective (such as content deliverer).

o Acknowledge that the role of facilitator of student learning is part of the job description.

o Work through a lesson planning scaffold or template that has within it boxes or places in which to insert active participation.

o Discuss with him how to deliver effective instructions for activities and ways to bring students back after the activity.

o Buy or see if his department can buy him a TeachTimer or similar device, so he can feel better about timing activities and then moving back to content.

- *Peer to peer*
  o Be sure she understands that her job description includes attending these meetings.

  o Think about ways to make the meetings more relevant to her and include her in planning the meeting.

  o Make sure to distribute notes after the meeting that clearly state each person's responsibilities and deadlines.

Question 6: What Resources Do You Need in Order to Successfully Carry Out These Strategies?

In this stage, consider what you need to have in place to be able to execute the strategies. Do you need funding? Books? Workshop schedules? Approval from someone at the district office? Those external resources will help you greatly so you can say, "I have looked into some support I can give you, and we have set up . . . ." Advanced planning is a great way to feel confident that you have done what you can to support your colleague to improve.

But to actually do the work, you need more than just external resources. You need self-awareness. Now that you have outlined strategies, what might stop *you* from putting them into action? Do you need more knowledge? The right words? Someone to work with as you move forward?

> What resources do you need to execute the strategies you outlined? What do you need to learn or relearn? What type of personal support do you need? What is your hunch about what emotion or value you need to tap into in order to be most effective?

At this stage, some people admit that they need courage. They need to be more flexible. They need to find more compassion within themselves. Whatever you decide, find support to help you locate your own needed resources. The hard conversation will take only a few minutes compared with the necessary support or supervision.

What do you need to get the job done?

Examples of Internal Resources

- *Supervisor to principal*
  - Have compassion for this individual's shift into a leadership position and the backbone one needs to build.
  - Show a sense of commitment by scheduling frequent times to meet to make sure the supervision is occurring.

- *Principal to teacher*
  - Find a way to schedule a coach or special education teacher to do some skill building around accommodations and lesson planning.
  - Be able to articulate a clear understanding of what needs to be accommodated.
  - Find time to observe the student in the next two months.
  - Find language around staff ownership rather than moving the problem back onto the special education teacher.

- *Coach to teacher*
  - Have compassion for the teacher wanting to stay within his comfort area in terms of teaching practices and not lose control of the classroom or move into an area of weakness.
  - Articulate your belief in the role of facilitator of student learning and some research or language around what active participation does for student learning.
  - Provide a packet of strategies for the teacher that fit his subject matter.
  - Seek out someone in the school in his subject area who would be open to being observed and discussing her lesson planning techniques with this teacher.

- *Peer to peer*
  - Be able to verbalize the impact on the team of your colleague not attending meetings.
  - Be able to speak without crying, chickening out, or getting overly emotional.
  - Be able to cite specific instances in which she hasn't done her job, rather than just a general sense that she hasn't.

SAMPLE OUTCOME MAPS

Here are three sample outcome maps. Look at the outcome maps to help you find words and suggestions in creating your own map.

Case One

A Physical Education Department Chair's Outcome Map

A physical education department chair was frustrated by a new colleague's behavior during the first quarter of school. Here is the outcome map she created to prepare herself for her hard conversation.

What Was the Presenting Problem?

The department chair was so frustrated, she initially found it difficult to articulate the problem. All she could say was that the teacher needed to "get with it." After some probing, she articulated that he had a lack of "understanding around specific protocols with regard to how the department managed unit planning and about the transition of fields and equipment from teacher to teacher."

What Was the Tentative Outcome?

She wanted him to "work effectively within the structures of the department for unit planning, lesson planning, and setting up playing fields."

What Desired Behaviors Would You Like to See and Hear?

The department chair wrote down four behaviors:

- Know what to bring with you to the specific field and make sure you have the equipment ready for that sport.
- Show up at 7:30 a.m. to set up your playing field early and be prepared.
- Follow the department chair lesson planning format.
- Show forward thinking by asking the department at least one week ahead about the unit you are about to do.

What Knowledge, Skills, and Dispositions/Attitudes Does This Person Need to Carry Out Those Behaviors?

Given that others in the department were very capable and able to execute the desired behaviors, what might have kept this teacher from doing so? The department chair was honest enough to say that the teacher

- needs to clearly know what is expected of him in terms of what time he is expected to show up,
- needs to know the required lesson plan format, and
- needs to see everyone in the department modeling these practices to understand that these expectations are common practice.

Then she added a disposition/attitude:

- needs to feel comfortable learning new tricks.

(Continued)

(Continued)

Knowing that her new faculty member had come to the profession as a second career and recently came from a different grade level, the department chair thought that he perhaps felt frustrated by the learning curve or by having new expectations placed on him. The department chair wanted to be more aware that this "new tricks" idea might or might not be a contributing factor to the situation.

What Strategies Can You Use to Promote This Person's Growth?

In particular, how would she communicate and work with her new teacher to facilitate the desired behavior change? She wrote:

- Articulate requirements verbally and in writing.
- Show him a sample lesson plan.
- Meet with the teacher weekly to review the plans, what he will need in terms of equipment, etc.
- Show the teacher what a prepared field looks like.
- Acknowledge how hard it is to be new and give positive feedback around whatever appears to be a challenging transitional piece for him.

What Resources Do You Need in Order to Be Successful in Carrying Out These Strategies?

The department chair paused at this point. Given that the strategies she articulated seemed manageable and quite straightforward, what might stop her from actually going forward? She said she needed

- help scripting the talk with the teacher, and
- courage to do the job.

Issues of age and gender were impacting her ability to follow through. She was younger and female, working with a second career male teacher, and she felt awkward at moments asserting her role. By sticking to a list of professional behaviors required of all teachers, no matter the individual's age or gender, the department chair felt more comfortable expressing her concerns.

Case Two

A Principal's Outcome Map

A principal watched a teacher struggling with the human side of teaching. Her relationship with students was robotic and stilted. While the principal knew the teacher cared for students, the teacher had a hard time expressing emotions in the classroom. The principal's outcome map helped her articulate her concerns.

What Is the Presenting Problem?

The teacher shows a lack of personal connection with students and has an uncomfortable presence in front of the classroom that seems robotic.

What Is the Tentative Outcome?

The teacher would have a more personal connection with students, more of a sense of belonging and welcome in the room.

What Would This Outcome Look Like and Sound Like?

The teacher would

- smile;
- appropriately share what she did over the weekend;
- acknowledge when she is aware a student participated in a sporting event, a school play, or other activity; if possible, attend school events;
- laugh with students;
- know students' backgrounds and, if applicable, ask students about the connection between their backgrounds and the material being studied;
- acknowledge the feelings in the room, for example, students are distracted by the upcoming senior prom, exhausted late on a Friday afternoon, or feeling tense about an upcoming test or project; assist the students in managing their anxiety or excitement.

What Knowledge, Skills or Dispositions/Attitude Would the Person Need to Have in Order to Do the Behaviors Embodied in the Outcome?

The teacher might need

- icebreaker techniques/get-to-know-you ideas for creating a sense of belonging in the class,
- permission to take time at the beginning of class to check in with students before jumping into the material,
- to feel comfortable self-disclosing to students,
- to want to know about students' lives and to be able to incorporate that knowledge into lesson plans, and
- to know it isn't always appropriate to lecture to students or to expect them to passively take notes.

What Strategies Would You Use to Help This Person Get to This Outcome?

- Provide observations of other teachers who have a more "at ease" classroom where students are sharing both personally and academically.
- Videotape the teacher to allow her to watch her engagement and relationship with all students.
- Articulate expectations around teacher behaviors—both in writing and verbal.

What Supports Do You Need in Order to Help You Implement the Strategies You Just Mentioned?

- Think about and possibly line up observations with teachers who have excellent personal connections with students.
- Make sure the video camera is on hand and tapes are available.
- If there are workshops in the area, check on dates and costs.
- Create a list of key teachers who create personal relationships in their classrooms (see Chapter 4 or Resource A and pick out key behaviors).
- Clarify in your own mind that this isn't simply a style difference. What is going on is truly impacting student learning.

Case Three

A Team Leader's Outcome Map

A team leader is finding it difficult to work with one member of her group. The colleague is making things uncomfortable for her team members with her tone of voice and her perceived unwillingness to work with others, whether parents or staff. Anticipating this issue would become an emotional challenge, the team leader used the map to stay professional and objective in her language.

What Is the Presenting Problem?

The teacher is ineffective in communication and lacks cooperation with peers, students, and parents.

What Is the Tentative Outcome?

The teacher would demonstrate effective communication with all parts of the community.

What Are the Desired Behaviors?

- Tone would be more approachable/softer.
- E-mails would be in proper format with attention to written style.
- Body language would not include furrowed brows, crossed arms, and lack of eye contact.
- Dress would be formalized beyond sweatshirt and sweatpants or jeans and more in alignment with the character of the district.
- The teacher would take feedback on collaborative behaviors and make changes.
- She would meet with counselors consistently (every few weeks).
- She would willingly participate in professional growth opportunities.
- She would make comments such as, "I will think about that . . ." and try to make changes in practice that align with feedback.

What Knowledge, Skills, or Disposition/Attitude Would the Person Need to Have to Implement the Behaviors Embodied in the Outcome?

The teacher might need

- self-confidence,
- awareness that a "tough girl" persona isn't serving her in her context, and
- ability to use appropriate language for a variety of situations.

What Strategies Would You Use to Help This Person Get to This Outcome?

- Provide written clear expectations.
- Ask the teacher what supports she wants.
- Provide observation feedback.
- Offer workshops if wanted.

What Supports Do You Need in Order to Help You Implement the Strategies You Just Mentioned?

- Review norms of group and group expectations with principal and with team.
- Get feedback from principal.
- Continue conversations such as this one with outsider observers.

CREATE YOUR OWN OUTCOME MAP

One principal I worked with commented, "This outcome map takes too long. We spent 25 minutes on my map. Given what I need to do at the school, I never have 25 minutes in a row to do something like this." I asked him how long he had had the problem. He replied, "Six months."

I hope you see that the 25 minutes spent trying to find solutions might have saved months.

Figure 5.1 provides a blank outcome map with its set of questions for your use.

People draw the map the way they think it will best work for them. Some create columns; others have created boxes. Whatever format you use, the key is to answer the questions in the order they are asked and *not to skip questions*. You must spend the time in the middle of the map before going to strategies in order to get the best work done.

Figure 5.1   Outcome Map

Outcome Map

1. *What is the presenting problem?*

   Paraphrase the problem and get it into a clear, concise statement.

   ```
   ┌─────────────────────────────────────┐
   │                                     │
   │                                     │
   │                                     │
   └─────────────────────────────────────┘
   ```

2. *What is the tentative outcome?*

   Articulate the solution concretely. What would you like to see happening instead of what is currently happening (existing state to desired state)? What is your best outcome?

   ```
   ┌─────────────────────────────────────┐
   │                                     │
   │                                     │
   └─────────────────────────────────────┘
   ```

3. *What would the employee's desired behaviors be if the problem were solved?*

   What specific and measurable things would you like to see or hear when the problem is solved? Keep the statement focused on *behaviors* one can see, hear, and repeat.

   ```
   ┌─────────────────────────────────────┐
   │                                     │
   │                                     │
   └─────────────────────────────────────┘
   ```

(Continued)

Figure 5.1 (Continued)

4. *What would the employee need to know and be able to do to implement the desired behaviors (internal resources)?*

   In order to implement these behaviors, what knowledge, skills, or awareness would this person need?

   | |
   | |

5. *What are some strategies you could use to help the person build up his or her resources and implement the desired behaviors?*

   What are some of the specific things you could do to address the needs? Given what you know about the person, what language or actions might help him or her with the desired behaviors?

   | |
   | |

6. *What are some of the resources you need in order to execute the strategies above (internal resources)?*

   In order for you to carry out the strategies, what do you need to learn or relearn? What type of personal support do you need? What is your hunch about what emotion or value into which you need to tap to be most effective?

   | |
   | |

SOURCE: Garmston & Wellman (1999, p. 235).

I THOUGHT THIS WOULD BE EASIER!

Around this point, some readers may be thinking, "I thought this hard conversation would be a lot easier. When I was done saying what I needed to say, the responsibility would be on the teacher to do it. This map has me doing this support and providing that resource. This is going to be harder than I thought."

Some educators are shocked after finishing the outcome map because they thought when they were done with the map, the work would be the other person's to complete. Not true. This map doesn't let you off the hook. Not only do you have to start the hard conversation, but you must be prepared to provide support as the strategies are implemented and to continue supervision and evaluation, if appropriate.

SUMMARY

The purpose of this chapter and working an outcome map was to help you clarify your expectations and to formulate an explicit and expedient plan to aid the person in meeting those expectations once you had the hard conversation. Just a few steps remain before you actually engage in your hard conversation. The scripting piece will begin in Chapter 6.

6

Scripting Your Initial Comments

The irony is this: If you don't go in . . . you can't find out.

—Richard Stine (1994)

It is not easy to speak up, find our voice, or tell our truths. Yet by doing so, we say yes to something bigger—what is best for schools, students, and ourselves. If we come from a sincere place, and we believe in the capacity of our colleague to hear us and for us to professionally discuss the issue, we are starting from the right spot.

I believe it was the right thing

- to tell my colleague not to read the newspaper during the training because it affected the way others could participate in the session and affected the trainer's ability to do her work.
- to tell a young teacher to manage her verbal contributions in a discussion because her voice was getting more airplay than others' voices were, and it wasn't right to dominate the discussion.
- to explain to someone up for tenure that her presence at district functions was expected and her lack of attendance showed poor judgment.
- to share with a colleague how her tone with students could be interpreted as intimidating and that students deserve an emotionally safe environment in which to learn.
- to talk to a colleague about how his inability to complete paperwork would get in the way of our work in a new teacher program and especially in the way of the teacher, who needed that documentation for his credential.

In all instances, what I was asking was that the teacher step up and be his or her best self. The role of the teacher is a daunting one to take on day in and day out. We don't wake up in the morning wondering if what we are doing is worthwhile or if we are doing good for the world. We are. It takes tremendous energy and courage and commitment to do the work of the educator. I honor the discipline and the dedication teachers and administrators have to the profession and to their students. In the rush of school day, we might forget how little decencies can have a big impact on our colleagues or how our work with students is so pivotal to their growth. We sometimes need a reminder and some support to be our best. It is with that intention that your script should be written.

GET CLEAR, CRAFT, COMMUNICATE: WHERE ARE WE?

We are finally at the communicating phase! This chapter on scripting will help you speak up in a way that makes you feel confident that you will be both supportive and clear in what you say. Then we will go on to talk about the *where*s and *when*s of communicating in Chapter 7 as well as think about additional types of hard conversation scripts in Chapter 8.

BEGINNING A SCRIPT

The most foundational pieces of a "good start" for a hard conversation include the following:

- Setting the tone and purpose of the conversation
- Getting to the point and naming it professionally
- Giving specific examples
- Describing the effect of this behavior on the school or colleagues or students
- Sharing your willingness to resolve the issue and have a dialogue and discussion

Write out these segments or pieces of the script as though you are completing a rough draft. Writing the words down will help you be sure you have all the parts. Once you are done writing, it is essential to read your script aloud to hear how it sounds.

Step 1: Set the Tone and Purpose of the Conversation

In the first sentence or two of the conversation, set the stage for the tone of the meeting. Like a doctor giving news to a patient, a financial advisor discussing the stock market, or a parent bringing up a difficult subject, tone makes a difference. Do you want to sound serious, but not tragic? Do you want to make the tone lighter than the conversation might feel to the person on the receiving end? What do you want to aim for in terms of feeling? These first few sentences set that most important tone.

If this is a serious matter that may involve the person losing this job, say so. If your concern should be considered just "food for thought" and the listener does not need to undertake any major action, say so. If you just wanted to clear the air and you don't expect a response, say so.

The point is that the other person should understand the intensity with which you are bringing up the issue, and yet you don't want them to hear more emotion than is intended. If you feel you need to offer a reassuring statement, do so.

These examples follow the scenarios from Chapter 5's outcome maps. Additional examples appear in Resource C.

- *Supervisor to principal*
  Susan, I know that your transition to being the principal has been challenging for you, and it isn't an easy thing to shift from being one of the teachers to being the one in charge, but I do need to talk to you about a key characteristic to being an effective principal.
- *Principal to teacher*
  Paula, you have been here a long time and you know your department looks to you for the institutional history you bring to the table, along with your fun projects and good humor. So this challenge you are having with Johnny is something that I have no doubt you will be able to resolve.
- *Coach to teacher*
  Rob, I know that you have great subject matter expertise. You are a whiz when it comes to high-level math and there's no question you love your content. We need to add another skill to your teaching repertoire for you to be an even better teacher.
- *Peer to peer*
  Mary, I know you have so many things on your plate this year with teaching and coaching and a new prep, and all of those obligations are important to you.

A Note About Investigatory Conversations

In some cases, you may need to bring up a difficult topic with someone as the supervisor, and yet you didn't witness the issue yourself. When you are going to ask someone about his or her behavior that you didn't see personally, you are having an *investigatory* conversation. These types of conversations are framed differently. Your purpose in an investigatory conversation is to gather information from the person about his or her perspective, and you must be clear that you were not the witness and are giving the individual some leeway.

- Julie, I want to talk to you about something I didn't personally witness but was told about. I appreciate your work with students, and you have always been a positive energy at our school, so I want to work with you to figure out what to do about . . .
- Tom, I know that you are a gifted math teacher and certainly care about your students and what you teach. So I can imagine that you will also be upset to know about something said to me. I am hoping we can work together to sort this out . . .

Be aware of when you are having an investigatory conversation rather than the hard conversations we will be working through here. The dialogue you are having in an investigatory conversation is tentative in language, firm but neutral. The conversation still needs to take place, but it needs to be done with both of you looking at the issue together as something to be "looked into."

Step 2: Get to the Point and Name It Professionally

This is where the professional language from Chapter 3 is helpful. As you name the issue, the "presenting problem" from your outcome map, watch for "trigger" words that will cause your listener to shut down. Listeners will immediately tune out the conversation if they hear phrases they perceive as personal affronts, such as, "You are being difficult," "Your class is chaotic," or "People think you are lazy." Stick to professional language that is not judgmental, and stay away from adjectives that will put people on the defensive.

These examples carry our scenarios to the next step:

- You haven't followed through on your responsibility to supervise and evaluate colleagues this year.
- Johnny needs additional accommodations during his time in your class.
- We need to talk about students having opportunities for more active participation in your class and how you can plan for this.
- You also have a responsibility to participate in our meetings.

Step 3: Give Specific Examples

At this stage, give one or two examples that illustrate the behavior or situation you want to change. Make sure that the examples are vivid enough that the person can clearly imagine them. For example, "Your lesson today was confusing for many," isn't as clear as, "I noted that 12 students asked you clarifying questions after you gave out the directions, and at least 5 of them continued to ask questions once you sent them back to do work."

Don't offer too many concerns at once. Not only will that be overwhelming for the listener, who will shut down, but it will also cause the listener to think "Boy, he has been watching me a long time. Why didn't he say something earlier?" Share the *most current* example or two with the individual. If you have noticed a pattern, describe it as succinctly as possible.

Look at these examples:

- In looking at your formal write-ups, I have noticed that you are missing several evaluations, especially for those teaching math and science. And in reviewing your priorities for this year, it seems that you have not observed the veteran teachers, although they are on your list for supervision.
- His parents say they have provided tutoring and changed his home situation around homework, but you need to change a few of your teaching behaviors as well, especially around checking for understanding and previewing and reviewing work with him during the week.

- In the last few observations, I have noticed that fewer than 50% of your students are doing any of the talking. You spend most of your time behind the overhead doing problems, and you don't provide much time for them to solve their own problems.
- You have sent me an e-mail the day of the meeting the last three times telling me you are going to be late or leave early, and one time you actually didn't show up.

Step 4: Describe the Effect of This Behavior on the School, Colleagues, or Students

This phrase or sentence attaches the purpose of the conversation. This is about impact and is the point where you describe the effect of this person's behavior on others. Perhaps your colleague did not recognize the consequence or social implication of the behavior in the school or community. If the teacher's job is at risk, share that fact in clear language at this time.

Review these examples in which the impact of the behavior on the school or students is explained:

- While it is awkward to give feedback to former colleagues, teachers notice your hesitance to take on all the responsibilities of the role and they feel freer to not be accountable for curriculum alignment or for deadlines. The ripple effect is that students don't get all of what they need in terms of curriculum or instruction.
- Johnny isn't feeling good about his work in social studies, and his transition to this grade level has left him lagging in grades. We need to boost him up and provide all we can so he has the ability to make it when he moves to the ninth grade. The impact of him not being successful here is just going to ripple into something none of us want for him.
- The problem is that the students are the ones who have to know the material and take the test, and they need time to practice during your class with you checking on their work.
- The effect on the group when one person doesn't come is huge. Your actions look to us like we aren't of value, and your absence gets in the way of us being able to align with you to make sure that all the students in our grade level get the same information. This lack of participation is hurting your relationship with your colleagues, and it's getting in the way of the consistency needed across classrooms.

Step 5: State Your Wish to Resolve the Issue and Open the Discussion

End the statement by indicating that you would like to see a change take place, and then ask for the listener's response. You could ask, How do you feel? How do you see this situation? What are your thoughts? Do you see this differently?

A wise administrator once said, "If you want to know how someone feels, do ask. But if you want simply to know if they understood what needs to happen next, ask if they understand and end it there." You choose the tone on which to end the statement, whether it is "hardball" or "softball."

Our sample scenarios conclude this way:

- I know the change to "boss" is a hard one, but it is needed. I am open to supporting you in the transition. What can I do?
- Given that we aren't going to do a pullout for him, and that the next steps regarding these accommodations are going to fall on you, I wanted to talk to you about what you need to do. Any thoughts?
- This is a huge shift in terms of what you've normally been doing, but it is what you need to do to support kids in their learning. Does this make sense to you?
- Can you see how this would affect us? What are you thinking?

Table 6.1 illustrates these foundational steps.

Table 6.1   The Foundational Steps

Five Steps to Successful Scripting	*Remember . . .*
Set the tone and purpose of the conversation.	Connection before correction—sincerity and willingness to be authentic precedes the rest.
Get to the point and name it professionally.	Name the issue with a professional behavior, preferably one indicated in a job description or expectation.
Give specific examples.	Use only one or two. Make them vivid and watch for trigger words.
Describe the effect of this behavior on the school, colleagues, or students.	Describe the consequences of this behavior on others. Don't dramatize; describe the impact.
Share your willingness to resolve the issue and have a dialogue and discussion.	Stay open with your comments and your body. Be able to finish your statement and stay present so the dialogue can begin.

ANNOTATED SCRIPTS

These scripts present the conversation from our scenarios in whole, so you can see how the pieces fit together. Additional examples are available in Resource C.

- Susan, I know that your transition to being the principal has been challenging for you, and it isn't an easy thing to shift from being one of the teachers to being the one in charge, but I do need to talk to you about a key characteristic to being an effective principal (SET THE TONE). You haven't followed through on your responsibility to supervise and evaluate colleagues this year (NAME THE ISSUE). In looking at your formal write-ups, I have noticed that you are missing several evaluations, especially for those teaching math and science. And in reviewing your priorities for this year, it seems that you have not observed the veteran teachers, although they are on your list for supervision this year (GIVE SPECIFIC EXAMPLES). While it is awkward to give feedback to former colleagues, teachers notice your hesitance to take on all the responsibilities of the role and they feel freer to not be accountable for curriculum alignment or for deadlines. The ripple effect is that students don't get all of what they need in terms of curriculum or instruction (DESCRIBE THE IMPACT). I know the change to "boss" is a hard one, but it is needed. I am open to supporting you in the transition. What can I do? (INDICATE A WISH TO DIALOGUE.)

- Paula, you have been here a long time and you know your department looks to you for the institutional history you bring to the table, along with your fun projects and good humor. So this challenge you are having with Johnny is something that I have no doubt you will be able to resolve (SET THE TONE). Johnny needs additional accommodations during his time in your class (NAME THE ISSUE). His parents say they have provided tutoring and changed his home situation around homework, but you need to change a few of your teaching behaviors as well, especially around checking for understanding and previewing and reviewing work with him during the week (GIVE SPECIFIC EXAMPLES). Johnny isn't feeling good about his work in social studies, and his transition to this grade level has left him lagging in grades. We need to boost him up and provide all we can so he has the ability to make it when he moves to the ninth grade. The impact of him not being successful here is just going to ripple into something none of us want for him (DESCRIBE THE IMPACT). Given that we aren't going to do a pullout for him, and that the next steps regarding these accommodations are going to fall on you, I wanted to talk to you about what you need to do. Any thoughts? (INDICATE A WISH TO DIALOGUE.)

- Rob, I know that you have great subject matter expertise. You are a whiz when it comes to high-level math and there's no doubt you love your content. We need to add another skill to your teaching repertoire for you to be an even better teacher (SET THE TONE). We need to talk about students having opportunities for more active participation in your class and how you can plan for this (NAME

THE ISSUE). In the last few observations, I have noticed that fewer than 50% of your students are doing any of the talking. You spend most of your time behind the overhead doing problems, and you don't provide much time for them to solve their own problems (GIVE SPECIFIC EXAMPLES). The problem is that the students are the ones who have to know the material and take the test, and they need time to practice during your class with you checking on their work (DESCRIBE THE IMPACT). This is a huge shift in terms of what you've normally been doing, but it is what you need to do to support kids in their learning. Does this make sense to you? (INDICATE A WISH TO DIALOGUE.)

- Mary, I know you have so many things on your plate this year with teaching and coaching and a new prep, and all of those obligations are important to you (SET THE TONE). You also have a responsibility to participate in our meetings (NAME THE ISSUE). You have sent me an e-mail the day of the meeting the last three times telling me you are going to be late or leave early, and one time you actually didn't show up (GIVE SPECIFIC EXAMPLES). The effect on the group when one person doesn't come is huge. Your actions look to us like we aren't of value, and your absence gets in the way of us being able to align with you to make sure that all the students in our grade level get the same information. This lack of participation is hurting your relationship with your colleagues, and it's getting in the way of the consistency needed across classrooms (DESCRIBE THE IMPACT). Can you see how this would affect us? What do you think? (INDICATE A WISH TO DIALOGUE.)

QUESTIONS ABOUT SCRIPTING

Additional questions commonly arise about scripting the hard conversation and how much emotion one should be expressing.

Should You Add Your Feelings to the Conversation?

If the professional behavior takes place in the classroom and has nothing to do with you or other colleagues, keep the discussion objective and factual. Talk about what you saw, not how you felt. By inserting your feelings into the mix it becomes an interpersonal concern, not a classroom concern. It isn't necessary to talk about how upsetting it is for you or how hurtful it is to observe a certain action in the classroom. If the concern is about the students, keep it that way.

For example, a teacher coach is dissatisfied with teachers in her school who are not providing what she feels English language learners need. Rather than expressing her frustration or anger, she can share with teachers what impact the lack of specific instruction in vocabulary is having on the students. The coach's frustration is important for her to note going into the conversation, but not nearly as important to share as the effect of the teachers' practices on students.

If the issue is interpersonal—about an interaction between you and the teacher—and you want to share that you were upset, you felt excluded, or you were saddened by a behavior, by all means do so.

On the other hand, if you contributed in any way to the situation yourself, you need to own up to that and mention your role. If your colleague says, "Well, you were there, too!" or "Didn't you also say back to me . . . ," then it will have been better to have admitted your own contributions to the problem at hand.

Deciding to talk about your feelings is a choice point in the scripting of the hard conversation. Base your choice on whether your feelings are relevant and will help make the teacher a better teacher.

What Is the Difference Again Between Intent and Impact?

Even if it is the truth we are going to tell, we are often reluctant to share bad news with someone because we truly believe he or she is good person. Hard conversations must happen with everyone, even nice people who bring brownies to the staff development day lunch or who bring coffee to their colleagues during a break. If there is something the person is doing that isn't serving students or is getting in the way of you and your school moving forward, you need to share that concern with them.

Teachers mean well and do things they think are good for kids. Without discounting that intent, we also need to recognize the facts of what happened as a result of the action. When the teacher does not allow late papers or makeup work, refuses to change the D- to a C+, or sends the student to the office, the effect may be far from what the teacher intended. It could be that the student didn't get the scholarship that would have allowed him to go to college, the child was berated at home again, the family won't allow the student to participate in the school musical, the only thing she was looking forward to. Our intentions may be honorable, but the effects of our actions need to be recognized as well.

WHAT WOULD YOU REWRITE? PRACTICING WITH ROUGH DRAFTS

Here are two additional scripts in rough draft form. These are initial drafts—they are not meant to be models of effective scripts—they are here to use as an exercise in better writing—edit them for what sounds right and what doesn't before you write your own script. Ask yourself what works, and more importantly, what doesn't. What would you change and why?

Rough Draft 1

Darryl, I want to talk to you about some concerns I have from observing your class. I want you to know as a veteran and experienced teacher on our staff that I value your work with our students. So I want to talk to you about this situation and work together on it with you.

I have observed that students are not engaged in your lessons, and there are some management issues we need to address. Today, I noted that students were not paying attention to your lecture, were coming in late to class unprepared with their homework, and this disrupting behavior wasn't addressed.

These issues are frustrating to watch, as classroom management is a key component of effective instruction. I am concerned that students are not receiving the optimal learning from your lessons, and at the same time I am concerned about the students' perception of your ability as an effective teacher.

I know I have noticed some of these issues before and apologize for not speaking to you about them sooner. I want to work with you in engaging students in learning by starting with improving classroom management.

I have been doing a lot of talking. Please share with me your perception about your classroom management and what you think about what I have noticed in your class.

Did You Have Similar Suggestions to the Following Edits?

Teachers who have taken my workshop gave the following suggestions to me. Do your edits look like theirs?

- Drop all of the comments about the students' perception of Darryl. It sounds like hearsay, and it takes the focus off what the colleague actually saw in the room and can comment about.
- Drop "it is frustrating to watch." It isn't important whether it was frustrating for the observer; what is important is what is affecting the students.
- Shorten it. Be sincere about valuing Darryl, but don't spend more than a sentence setting this up. Apologize in a phrase. Edit this down to about five sentences. It "feels" like it goes on too long.

Possible Second Draft

Darryl, I know you want what is best for all kids, so I want to talk to you about observing some of your students not engaged in your lesson today.

While observing, I noted that some students were not paying attention to your lecture, and some were coming in late to class unprepared with their homework, yet you didn't address these behaviors.

Not addressing these behaviors might be getting in the way of you offering an optimal learning environment to all the students. What's your take on what I saw from my perspective?

Rough Draft 2

Kristin, I want to speak to you about the specifications of your job. I appreciate all you do for the school and that you take on additional responsibilities. However, I need to talk to you about the boundaries of your job description. You went outside the boundaries of your job description when you informed the counselor and the psychologist that they were going to be switching offices. This was unexpected information for them and it was not to come from you. It isn't part of your job to discuss those types of situations with anyone. When you give information that is outside your purview, it creates an inaccurate perception that I have given you permission to share certain details and carry out certain tasks when I have not. As leader of this school, I can't have those perceptions out there. I want to support you and resolve this issue because you offer so many positives to the school.

What are your thoughts?

Did You Have Similar Suggestions to the Following Edits?

Here's what educators said about this script.

- Needs editing. Shorten it.
- Needs greater clarity, clearer verbs.
- Be more positive and supportive.
- Too stilted in tone.

Possible Second Draft

Kristin, you do great work for our school and I want you to keep doing that great work, so I need to talk to you about what I perceive is a stepping-out-of-bounds situation that happened last week. You informed the counselor and the psychologist that they were switching offices, and it wasn't information for you to share. Certain communications need to come from me, and when you share information that isn't to be shared by anyone other than me, it creates the inaccurate perception that that information was yours to offer. You do such good work that I want to clear up this communication slip and get really clear as to what is and isn't appropriate for you to communicate so we can get back to being on track. Make sense? What do you think?

QUICK SCRIPTS

The scripts we've analyzed—like the outcome maps in the previous chapter—may intimidate some readers who fear that it will take many hours to achieve the perfect combination of words. Rest assured that scripting gets easier with time,. But if the sample scripts in this chapter seem overwhelming and you would prefer to start small, refer to the following samples. It may be possible to say what you need to say in three sentences or less. Perhaps some of the following ideas will work for you.

State My Path

Kerry Patterson and coauthors of *Crucial Conversations* (2002) outline a "State My Path" script that contains three sentence stems. Use this type of script when you want to immediately share the impact that someone has had on you. If you just felt an "ouch" during a meeting or watched a teacher-student interaction that you thought was hurtful, you can describe it in these three sentences.

1. "This is what I have noticed . . . ." State the behavior or action that just took place.

2. "I am beginning to think or feel . . . ." Describe your feeling or interpretation of what the impact was.

3. "Is this what you meant?" Invite the person to share his or her perspective on what just happened.

For example, having just seen what I believed was a harsh and possibly harmful interaction between my colleague and a young student, I might say the following:

"Matt, I noticed you said, 'What do you want?' in a gruff way when this student came to see you at your desk. If I were that girl, I might feel intimidated about coming to ask you a question if I got that kind of response when I came into the teacher's office. Did you sense that she was a bit shy in responding to you and might not feel comfortable? Can you see that?"

I-Message Feedback Statements

Andrea Corney (2004), an organizational consultant, has two other scripts she calls "I-Message Feedback Statements." These are used during interpersonal communication moments when there has been a "pinch" and you want to clear it up so that you remain focused in the present. It requires great self-monitoring, thinking on one's feet, and managing one's tone, but if we all practiced this type of communication more often, we wouldn't hold onto hurts from previous encounters and bring the past into current situations so consistently.

The first message has two simple parts:

1. "When you do (behavior), I think/feel (reaction)."

2. "It would be helpful to me if you could do (behavior) instead. Would that work for you? What do you need?"

For example, in dealing with a colleague who has been late to the last three meetings, I might say the following:

When you come to our meeting late, I get the sense that the meeting isn't important to you and that leads me to think you discount the group's work in some way. I don't know if it is true, but it would be helpful to the group and me if you could show up on time. Is there something I can do on my end to facilitate this?

A second I-message script offers your perspective in asking for change:

"Here is the problem as I see it. What is going on from your perspective?"

"What am I doing that gets in the way?"

"What can we both do to fix this problem?

For example, I'm working together at a department meeting with a grouchy veteran colleague. I might say the following:

When you roll your eyes and respond to my comments in the brainstorm with "Yeah, but . . . ," I have to admit I get angry and pretty much shut down. I have no idea if you know you are doing this, but it is impacting me. I would really like to be able to participate in this meeting without feeling bad about it. Can you see this from my perspective?

NOW PUT ASIDE THE SCRIPT

You may be left with the impression that scripting is very academic and prescriptive. Remember that scripting is meant to be a *starting* point for you, but it is not the absolute formula for success. Remember, success in these conversations is about authenticity, sincerity, and working from the stance that as professionals, we are obligated to have these conversations for the sake of our schools and our students. Don't let a scaffolding tool get in the way, but instead use it if you feel it is helpful and can support you in communicating what you feel is important to be said.

A key point: Do not bring the script with you.

When you go to have your hard conversation, leave the script at home. Yes, this is scary, but needs to be done. You've put a lot of effort into crafting this conversation. But imagine someone coming to you with two pages of a typed monologue. The natural reaction is to feel intimidated and defensive. Besides, reading your script from a paper would be inauthentic and would limit your ability to have a meaningful, in-the-moment conversation. An even worse case scenario is that your piece of paper inadvertently falls into the wrong hands and is used against you.

Memorize the gist of what you want to say. Don't worry about memorizing every line or making sure the entire paragraph comes out of your mouth in perfect form. Rarely do moments that are full of emotion and anxiety come out perfectly in real life. You have your outcome map strategies in your head. You know how you will support the teacher when the time comes to discuss next steps. Don't check your heart at the door. If your intentions are good, you have conscientiously thought through the issue, you are committed to continued dialogue, you are open to alternative ways of looking at the changes to be made, and you honor and respect the other person as a professional, then your initiation of this conversation will come across as authentic and will be a successful start to the dialogue.

SUMMARY

This chapter took you closer to having your conversation by providing you with scripting strategies and examples to help ensure that you have started off on the right foot. The following chapter explores the logistics of conversations beyond the meaning of your words.

7

The *Whats,*
Wheres, and
Whens of
Having a Hard
Conversation

Excellence is in the details. Give attention to the details and excellence will come.

—Perry Paxton

The words are in your head, the outcome map is in your metaphorical back pocket, and now you need to find the opportunity to speak. You have your clarity, you've crafted your conversation, and now it's time for the final C—communication.

What are the best locations for having a hard conversation? Are there better times to say something difficult? How do we get to the point of having the conversation? How do we let the other person know we want to talk? While we might never find a perfect time to speak up, there are certainly less than opportune times and locations.

I once knew a first-year teacher who was insecure about her teaching and somewhat wary of her principal. One Friday afternoon, she got an e-mail from the principal that said, "We need to talk Monday morning." She was extremely upset. She went home and thought about possible meanings for the note until she literally threw up. And all the principal really wanted was to check in with her on how she was feeling about her first year.

Considering several factors makes the chances of having a better conversation more likely.

PREPARING THE LOGISTICS

Initiating the Contact

Cryptic voice messages or e-mails that leave the recipient without any ideas about the topic of the conversation are less than a good beginning, as with that first-year teacher. Particularly if you are a supervisor, be certain to determine the best time and place for this conversation and be prepared to conduct yourself with the utmost professionalism. Teachers will remember if they were caught off guard or thrust into a conversation. When I need to discuss a sensitive subject with a peer, having a private space to conduct a conversation without others listening makes me feel most at ease.

Finding a Location

Where should you have the hard conversation? In the teacher's classroom? In your office? In a neutral space? What messages are you sending by having the conversation in any of these locations?

To put your colleague more at ease, consider the classroom or that person's office. It is a space in which he or she is most comfortable, and you are traveling to their turf, which might make the conversation easier.

If you are trying to send a message of formality and set a more serious tone, invite the teacher or employee to your office. We all have memories of someone being sent to the principal's office and what that location meant for us. Will your conversation be associated with punitive action? Supervisors should choose the location and seating arrangement very consciously.

Be aware of how furniture and location affect people's level of comfort. Once the teacher or employee is inside the office and the door is shut, where will you sit? Behind your desk? Putting a desk between yourself and the person establishes a sense of power for you and a sense of vulnerability for the individual. Sitting at a circular table or putting yourself in a chair at the teacher's side creates a different feeling, one more of collaboration and equal status.

As a coach, I find it helpful to go to a teacher's room where we can shut the door rather than trying to say anything difficult in a staff room or a department office where colleagues are just a moment away from opening the door or hearing over the cubicle wall. Using a private space during a prep period always helps. My former supervisor, if the issue wasn't terribly difficult, would often try to find a way to walk somewhere with me—whether it was to get something in his room or to walk to the office—to get us out and moving.

Thinking About Timing

Is there a best time of day to talk to someone? Different circumstances might affect your choice of the day and time. Consider the following:

- Does the employee or colleague have to teach or work directly after this conversation?
- Am I allowing enough time for this conversation?
- Am I allowing enough post-conversation time for the person to have more than a minute to process before he or she needs to work with children, go on yard duty, teach, and so on?

Having a conversation with someone on a Friday gives him or her the 48 hours of the weekend to contemplate the discussion or cool off. They also may get angry in that time and call every one of their colleagues to stir up some drama for Monday morning.

Some suggest Tuesday or Wednesday for difficult conversations. By allowing a few days to informally see the person, one can check in again before the weekend for any additional steps.

With the outcome map and the action plan in place, the initial conversation was only that—a first talk—so allowing for another check before the weekend shows the teacher or employee that he or she will be supported and that additional follow-up actually will take place. While it is true that certain hard conversations take only one time in order for things to change, most conversations are ongoing. They will require some follow-up and support.

Remembering Body Language: Voice, Hands, Eyes

Think about how you will use tone and body language during the hard conversation. Using a "credible" voice, your tone goes down at the end of a sentence. A credible voice conveys authority; the tone gives the impression that you know what you are talking about. When you use an "approachable" voice, also called "up speak," your tone goes up at the end of the sentence, and the listener is less likely to have a sense that you feel any strength of conviction. The listener may be less likely to take you seriously, but also may be less threatened.

You can achieve the same sense of authority or approachability with the placement of your hands. Michael Grinder (2007) says putting your palms down as you discuss the situation is a cue that you mean business. Putting your hands palms up offers the observer or listener an opening, a welcome, and an invitation to join in the conversation more freely.

Eye contact is another body language signal to be aware of. In some situations, not looking at someone may indicate hesitation, but looking too intently may be imposing. It is up to you to consider the cultural implications of eye contact and how your listener will perceive it. As with all verbal and body language, we perceive it through our filters of perception, through our cultural backgrounds, and through what we have been taught by our upbringing. Be aware of how you come across. By not seeming too shy or too threatening, you will achieve a middle ground that is effective for your situation.

THINKING ABOUT YOUR LANGUAGE

In *Survival of the Savvy: High-Integrity Political Tactics for Career and Company Success*, Rick Brandon and Marty Seldman (2004) discuss weak and harsh vocabulary. Just as your body language triggers a reaction, your words can lead someone to perceive you as weak or strong, and these judgments occur in seconds and with just one phrase.

Brandon and Seldman break down language into two categories. In the weak language category, you say things that make you seem tentative ("kind of"), apologetic ("I hate to bother you"), self-discounting ("You probably won't agree with me, but . . ."), ambivalent ("I might be wrong"), or vague ("Parents have said . . .").

Using phrases in the harsh language category might have you appear autocratic ("I am not asking you; I am telling you"), opinionated ("The facts plainly show"), critical ("This is a waste of my time"), blaming ("If you'd paid attention"), or prone to exaggerate ("Anyone can see . . .").

> ### Phrases to Consider
>
> Here are a few comments that have worked for others in the past. Review them and see if they'd fit your situation.
>
> "Let me press you a bit about . . ."
>
> "I would like to plant a seed . . ."
>
> "Can I challenge you on a point?"
>
> "I believe you don't intend to teach in an inequitable way, so let's try to make your actions align with your intentions."
>
> "I have been sitting with something for a while and it isn't going away, so I feel I need to share it with you."

Being mindful of these short, but powerful phrases can help you be heard in the way you intended. Clarity is key in a hard conversation, so pay attention and don't use other trigger words such as *frequent, numerous, chaotic, unorganized,* or *unclean.* Exact numbers or specific examples are much more effective. Watch out for any words that may be considered too broad or general or those that can't be backed up with specifics.

A colleague wanted to talk to a teacher about a concern she had. The two agreed they would talk. The first woman e-mailed the teacher then and suggested that she had time to talk and could "accommodate" her by meeting that afternoon. Listen to the trigger word! This teacher wanted to engage on an equal level with her colleague, yet the colleague created a hierarchy and a sense of power by saying she could "accommodate" her peer. The meeting never took place.

Another of the key language mistakes many of us make is not being clear enough and thinking that we were. In many situations, the expectation is on the listener to figure out that we really mean business. We expect people to understand this "code." You're really saying, "I mean it!" but your words are, "You might want to consider . . ."

Many of my colleagues, especially those of the Boomer generation, born from 1946–1964, understand this code and expect that others do as well. They may feel like it's uncouth and too direct to say things bluntly. They expect others to understand.

Well, unfortunately, that isn't the case. Many newer teachers in the field aren't working under the same presuppositions. Corporate America has been working for some time with the idea of being generationally savvy, and in that time, consultants, bloggers, and career coaches also have focused on generational differences at work. In the field of education, one of the key differences among the generations is in the use of language. Boomers, being 80 million strong, needed to learn how to compete and work with one another without offending. They "read between the lines" when it comes to feedback. Gen Xers (those born between 1964 and 1980) expect more direct feedback of the sort that makes Boomers uncomfortable. Gen Xers grew up with more "truth" coming at them, both in the home with single parents and on TV with more transparency in government and more real-time coverage of the world, on CNN, for example. Gen Xers expect this precision and clarity in their work communication too.

Educational consultant Andy Platt and others (2000) discuss how the words *recommendation*, *suggestion*, and *expectation* are perceived differently. A Boomer would pick up a "recommendation" from an evaluation and immediately work to make that recommendation a reality. Those in the next generation need "expectations" or "nonnegotiables." For them, this is not too blunt or rude. It is clear. If you offer a "suggestion," make it be something that the person may act on or not.

Millennials, our newest teachers born between 1980 and 1994, are the products of our praise awards, "Student of the Month" bumper stickers, middle school "bucks" or "pats on the back," and certificates for anything and everything. They expect clear guidelines and feedback spelled out.

To communicate successfully, we must not assume the listener can read between the lines or infer our meaning from our tone. We must get comfortable with spelling out what we would like to see happen.

Phrases to consider are examined in Table 7.1.

Table 7.1   Phrases to Consider Regarding Clarity of Expectations

Ineffective wording	Effective wording
Perhaps you should . . .	The expectation is . . .
You might consider . . .	This is not negotiable . . .
I would encourage you to . . .	Please begin to implement . . .
A thought I have is . . .	You are required to . . .
Something you might want to . . .	Please do the following . . .

PROPS FOR THE MEETING

Many of my colleagues who are nervous about having the hard conversation feel more in control when they have their lines written out and with them. It just isn't worth it. Do your best, know as much as you can, and as I have said before, leave the script at the door. Memorize the first few lines and the key concepts and leave it at that.

You may want other materials, however, in the meeting. Do you want to have the teacher or employee leave with anything in writing? Is there data someone needs to look at—a grade printout, an e-mail to which you need to refer? Bring that type of information.

Michael Grinder (2007), an expert in nonverbal communication, found that sometimes having a "third point," something in writing that you and your colleague both are looking at, can decrease the tension between you (the first point) and the other person (the second point).

Having less eye contact during difficult moments frees up people to discuss the topic at hand. Parents recognize this when they wait until they are in the car, eyes forward and driving before they initiate that awkward conversation with their children. The same is true with certain situations with colleagues.

If you are a supervisor working with a principal or a classified staff member, you may want to use as a focal point the administrative standards for your state or your district or the job description for the classified staff member that comes from the human resources office. If the discussion is about an expectation that has not been met, having that specific document stating the expectation in writing can allow you and your colleague to look down and review the document rather than looking at each other.

At other times, eye contact is the better choice. Eye contact makes a different statement and may increase the person's anxiety level, which may be the wake-up call you intended. You must decide the message you want to send.

PREPARING EMOTIONALLY

I worked with an administrator for many years who had a tendency to tease and be downright snippy. It made me so anxious to work for him that I chose to say something about it during one of our appointments. I went to the gym that morning and jogged fast, put on one of my favorite outfits for flair and wore a pendant for good luck. On my way to the meeting, I listened to some empowering rock music, and during the meeting, although I might have looked silly, I bet I held on to that pendant. All of my preparations gave me that little boost of confidence I needed to get through the conversation, and my colleague certainly hasn't been as disrespectful in our meetings since.

Some of us need to prepare ourselves emotionally as the final step in readying ourselves for the meeting. Are you one of them? If you are, ask yourself the following questions:

- Do I have a way to hold onto my energy in the face of resistance?

- Do I have a coping strategy if the other person cries or gets angry?

You can psyche yourself up for a conversation by

- getting a good night's sleep,
- going to the gym and working out that morning,
- dressing professionally,
- listening to empowering music, or
- wearing a charm or something you can squeeze in moments of stress.

DURING THE CONVERSATION

As hard as it might be, try to sit silently after you have spoken. Don't keep talking just because you are uncomfortable. It is awkward to have a hard conversation, and once the person initiating has said a few words, many of them just keep talking because they don't like the silence. Not a good idea. The other person needs silence to be able to join in. Or the listener might have been joining in all along, but it's time to leave the "air space" free for the listener to respond. You will need internal fortitude and to cultivate a sense of strength to stop, but silence is, in many instances, the best choice. Smothering, excusing, apologizing, or getting in the way with your voice or a touch won't be as helpful as being quiet and allowing the other person to "take it in."

You may need to sit on your hands, casually put your hand over your mouth, change the position in your chair, put your arms to the side, or give yourself a signal to stop yourself from interfering with the other person's moment to manage his or her reaction. This doesn't mean you can turn away, fold your arms in a "So there!" position, or put a scowl on your face. You need to maintain a connection with the listener and keep open a channel to continue the discussion, but you just don't want to jump across the net and manage their response as well.

What if the person starts to cry? Say "I can see you need to process this information. I am happy to sit here until you feel ready, or we can reschedule for some other time today or tomorrow. Does tomorrow after school seem like a good time for you?" It's fine to have to reschedule for a time when both of you can feel prepared.

I once sat in on a meeting between two colleagues that became quite emotional. One person needed to share her frustration and hurt over a decision she had thought was selfish. This colleague had brought me in to make sure both sides were heard and that the meeting wouldn't become a "she said; no, she said" scenario. The first woman shared her concern in a professional manner. The listener, shocked and I imagine a little chagrined, began to weep. She cried throughout the 20 minutes we were all together, but it did not stop her from having the conversation. She was simply experiencing the emotion. We sat there as she then shared her side of the story. My colleague who initiated the conversation continued to engage with her peer as an adult and calmly provided tissues. Holding someone accountable for being professional, even through his or her tears, can be the responsible thing to do.

Many people can handle tears, but are tripped up by anger. One principal with an anger problem was known to not just fume—he screamed. Some people seethe, squint, and seem very scary to others. Other people yell and are very verbal. This man was a yeller, but his colleagues summoned the courage to tell him he wasn't doing himself any favors by being so intimidating or impulsive. Ultimately, it was suggested to him that he take another position. At that point, he took a hard look at how his behaviors had affected his professional relationships and his career path.

If the person begins to yell, it's perfectly appropriate to say, "If we can't talk about this professionally, I will need to end this meeting and we will need to reschedule for another time."

If you feel too anxious about the tone or the volume, or if someone gets up and starts shoving or hitting objects, try to hold your center. If the situation begins to seem unsafe, by all means remove yourself.

CONVERSATIONAL STYLES

Colleagues give me scenarios and say, "What should I do with a person who is chatty or someone who clams up?" or "What should I be mindful of when speaking to an individual who is like this . . . ?" While every conversation is unique and some suggestions might not fit for everyone, here are a few suggestions for working with people who have a variety of communication styles.

Person 1: I love the arts, am very creative, emotional, and intuitive; I need ways to process information other than reading or writing.

To talk with this person you might consider these suggestions:

- Think about sitting at a couch or a circular table to create a personal connection.
- Think about doing some writing in the meeting to outline key ideas in bullets.
- Think about body language—consider opening up your body, facing the person, having a calm look on your face; crossing your arms and looking down doesn't create the safety that this emotional person might need in order to truly hear you.
- Follow up with e-mail and deadlines—consider that some people might still be dealing with their feelings when you are done so that any specific details or requirements you have left with them might not have been duly noted. You might consider writing something down for them (keep it short and sweet) so they have something to refer back to if the memory of the conversation is blurry.

Person 2: I am the one to depend on for the right answer and to bring insight into a situation. You need to challenge me, push me to stretch.

　　To talk with this person you might consider these suggestions:

- Think about pressing her to build her repertoire and flexibility.
- Think about helping her increase her influence and capability.
- Ask her to think about "What sort of an impact might there be if . . ."
- Offer her time for processing.
- Ask for her thoughts, and truly listen.

Person 3: I am a person who tends to listen more than I talk. It isn't that I don't know the answer. Just don't push me or put me on the spot.

　　To talk with this person you might consider these suggestions:

- Have the conversation in a safe spot, such as the teacher's room.
- Offer lots of silent time.
- Watch your use of harsh vocabulary.
- Plan for more than one follow-up conversation.

Person 4: I am a confident person who appreciates candidness. You cannot reach me through songs and fun games. I need you to speak to me as an adult.

　　To talk with this person you might consider these suggestions:

- Don't use patronizing language; keep credible and neutral.
- Outline explicit expectations.
- Keep calm in the face of resistance and arm crossing.
- Consider meeting earlier in the week, at the end of the day, and in your own office.

Person 5: I am a person who has a hard time focusing. I am worried about my personal life. I need you to care about me as a person before I will listen to you as a professional.

　　To talk with this person you might consider these suggestions:

- Take notes during the session and possibly follow up with an e-mail too.
- Be mindful of your body language and use your approachable voice.
- Consider the top one or two changes you want to make and focus on what can be done.
- Work with asset-building language and avoid harsh vocabulary.
- Make small encouraging comments and use positive reinforcement.

Person 6: I am a person who loves to talk in order to process. I need you to help me find my voice and when to use it. I need a place to express myself verbally.

To talk with this person you might consider these suggestions:

- Set strong parameters around the way you will communicate during the meeting. Say, "I want to say a few things. It would help if I could get those out without interruption, and then I am happy to answer any questions and listen."
- Set aside some time for this conversation as there is most likely much this person needs to process. Give it more time than you might think just in case.

THE BIGGER YES

People have asked me what happens if the person completely discounts your comments and leaves in a huff. How does one regroup and try again if the conversation topic truly is one that must be addressed? This situation is rare but is everyone's biggest fear. If you are in a position of authority, much can be done that is beyond the scope of this book—not comfortable actions, but actions that go into the legal side of hiring and firing with documentation and proper paperwork.

What if you don't have formal authority, don't feel comfortable bringing it in, and still you feel the need to regroup and speak up? This is where strength in your purpose needs to drive you. For you to go back to this person and ask, "Are you willing to talk about the students at this point?" or "Are you willing to consider other options?" or "Is this a better time to talk about what happened?" we need a bigger *yes* backing us up.

William Ury (2007) terms it as the "ultimate yes." Whatever this bigger picture *yes* is for you—be it better teaching for all students, a better working climate for all employees, better adult-to-adult communications in the school—these are some of the *yes* rewards we are working toward. Is it being able to feel comfortable knowing you have done everything you can to make the school an identity-safe place for all kids? Is it that you can sleep better at night knowing that you tried not once but many more times than just once to remind others that to be our best selves we need to communicate in a professional manner? What goal are you trying to reach with your hard conversation?

What is the greater *yes* you are aiming for in your hard conversation? Knowing that the conversation may be emotional or rocky for a short time can be OK if you remember what you are striving to accomplish. Knowing what your greater *yes* is helps you deal with the current discomfort.

SUMMARY

While you can't control every detail of the environment in which you have the hard conversation, this chapter hopefully assisted you in considering those aspects that you can influence and adjust in a way that makes the situation a little less challenging for both of you. The next chapter looks at other types of hard conversations we haven't considered yet.

8

What If?
Other Types of
Hard Conversations

Being grown up is a terribly hard thing to do. It is much easier to go from one childhood to another.

—F. Scott Fitzgerald

There are so many other hard conversations we find ourselves needing to have that go beyond the tools already presented, so many challenges, moments, and awkward situations that come our way. Oftentimes, we find ourselves stuck.

Here are a few additional thoughts for some of those moments.

What if Your Hard Conversation Is With a Large Group Instead of One Person?

Principals, curriculum coordinators, and administrators often need to kick off new initiatives that may or may not be welcomed, move a change effort forward that is possibly unwanted and unsolicited, or speak to an angry faculty full of hurt feelings. What might help when it comes to addressing a whole group versus just one other person?

- Put together a tight agenda in which you acknowledge where you are as a group and where you need to be, and then keep the conversation moving from the existing state of affairs into the desired state. In this way, the group moves beyond blame or accusations and is asked to be proactive, to spend their energy on what to do to reach the goal.

- Addressing the concern with a staff directly may be the best move, but it might be better if you had a facilitator for the meeting. When do you use a facilitator? Invite a facilitator if you are too emotional or you think the group might feel safer with someone leading the meeting and keeping structure.
- The same key components involved in individual conversations (explicit professional behaviors, mapping, watching for trigger words, body language, etc.) continue to need attention.

This district office administrator story emphasizes her use of body language and direct acknowledgment of the issue at hand to move past resistance.

I needed to do some training around a topic that the group wasn't too keen on. Most of the staff wasn't interested in staff development to begin with; others specifically didn't think it would address their needs. I had heard rumors that specific people were calling it a waste of time, and that was saying it kindly.

I began the session by acknowledging that some people might think this was a topic that wasn't important to their practice or that it might be something that wasn't useful to the school, and I put my palm out to face the door of the room, implying that I wasn't accusing anyone inside the room but that I had heard things outside this room before I got here. Then I moved into the room a few more steps, directed eyes to my PowerPoint, and said, "However, there are some challenges that many of us do face with regard to this topic . . ."' and I cited them on the slide. No one could disagree with my facts. I ended this difficult 60 seconds by moving into the room toward my audience one step more, looking directly at them and saying, "And today we are going to talk about how to deal with it."

I didn't pull any punches. I reported to them what I had heard the naysayers saying, described that there was indeed something wrong, and told them we were going to work on solving it. The rest of the morning went without a hitch.

What if You Need to Address Your Superior?

In these situations, think *permission* and *influence*. Ask the individual's permission to offer suggestions or difficult feedback. Instead of coming out with, "I need to tell you what I am feeling" or "We need to talk about how things are going in this department," you might consider asking a question before offering a statement. Here are a few opening lines to try:

- "Are you open to hearing a few ideas about communication among the staff?"
- "Would you be interested in some thoughts I have about how to increase your influence with the teachers?"
- "I am willing to do what you have suggested. Are you willing to consider other options?"

In these situations you are asking for permission to offer your thoughts and suggestions. As an aside, consider using the word "I" in your comments rather than taking yourself out of the initial question. Ideas *you* have instead of just talking about ideas in general may be more welcome.

If your supervisor is not open or interested in listening at that specific time, so be it. If you sense that your timing isn't right rather than the person not being interested in the conversation, perhaps wait and try to find another entry point later. By asking permission, you get access when the listener might be truly ready to receive the feedback, and that is a much better place from which to begin.

This new teacher coach at a suburban school district shares a story in which she spoke up to her administrator on behalf of her colleagues.

We had just gone through the process of interviewing for a position on our coaching team. My supervisor had been given the responsibility for calling those interviewees who did not get the job. It was the end of the year and with a lot on her plate before school ended, she ended up leaving messages or talking on her cell phone to the teachers in crowded places. It left a strong impression on those who received the calls. They felt dismissed and disrespected, and I heard about it.

Knowing that this process would happen again in the future, I wanted to make sure she was aware of the difficulties these teachers had experienced when getting those calls. My conversation went something like, "I know you had a tight deadline in terms of getting back to teachers about the position and that you completed your job. I have received some feedback on how it could have been done even more smoothly. Are you open to hearing it right now?" There was a long pause on the other end and then, having thought through how ready she was for feedback, she said she was.

I was factual and discussed the impact her choices on how and when to give the bad news by cell phone during rush hour had had on those receiving it. I didn't have the task or authority she did, but my colleagues felt comfortable enough to share their feelings with me, so I did have the information—and it needed to get to her. I think asking for permission to share it was the best first step.

> ### "Give Three"
>
> Once you have the ear of the supervisor and you are hoping to change his or her mind on a given issue, you might want to provide a list of possible alternative ideas for him or her to choose from. Educational consultants Laura Lipton and Bruce Wellman (2001) have the "Give Three" approach. Lipton and Wellman suggest that offering only one suggestion doesn't give the listeners enough choice and they won't feel freed up to actually pick something that'll fit for them. They must either take the one idea or none. Offering only two suggestions limits thinking, and the listeners might side with the second alternative or whichever one you emphasize as the better choice. By giving your supervisor three suggestions, you make them true suggestions, and offer your supervisor an authentic alternative choice that will suit both of you.

What if You Feel That You Are Doing More Than Your Share of the Work and You Feel Responsibilities Are Not Being Evenly Divided?

Good question. I think one needs to consider with whom this conversation needs to be—your supervisor, who perhaps has control over who is doing which tasks, or with your colleague. Is this a conversation about reallocating your time because you've realized since some responsibilities are taking more time or are more complex that those of your colleagues, you need fewer tasks due to these larger tasks being more difficult? Or is this an issue of your colleague not following through on tasks that have been given to her and you feel for the good of the group you need to do her job and yours as well so it will just get done? Those are two very different conversations. Be politically savvy and determine which conversation you need to have. Keep your emotions out of it. Discuss the facts, the behaviors, and the impact this inequity of job responsibilities is having on you and the organization. You may come to find out that your strengths lie in one place and your colleague's in another and you need to reassign tasks. Or you may find your administrator had no idea what the time commitment is for doing the job. Presume positive intentions and be clear that you are not trying to shirk your responsibilities, but that you'd discuss this now and keep your two feet in the present. Becoming angry and resentful as a result of feeling that you are doing other people's work just makes for an unhappy work climate.

What if You Feel You Are Being Asked to Do Something by Your Supervisor That You Feel Is Inappropriate?

A management consultant colleague who works with the armed forces told me once that if a member of the armed forces was asked to do a task that could cause harm, he or she *must* speak up and say something to the superior officer, such as "Sir, do you realize that if we do move this boat in that direction by that many degrees we will hit an iceberg?" If the supervisor at that time says, "Yes, I do," it is the responsibility of the crew member to move that ship. Because that crew member spoke up, if the ship hits that iceberg, the responsibility rests with the superior officer, not the crew member. If the crew member hadn't spoken up, his or her job would also be on the line. Even those in the lowest of hierarchical positions must voice their concerns.

While we do not literally hit icebergs in our line of work, there will certainly be moments when we hit them metaphorically. I hope through reading this book you have become stronger and more capable in articulating what you as an educator stand for and feel others should be doing in schools for students. Talk to your supervisor about her suggested inappropriate actions and set forth in front of her the possible consequences and impacts that the behavior would cause. If you feel that you aren't being heard, and work in a public school system, you could seek support with your union. If not, and you have someone who does the work of a human resources officer, go talk to that person. The levels of impropriety are many, and looking into what is insensitive, inappropriate, or illegal would be a good thing to do.

What if an Issue Gets Blown Up by Group E-mails? How Do You Stop It?

As mentioned in the etiquette section in Chapter 4, each school or organization should have some norms about e-mail communication so that all group e-mails are monitored and used only for specific business. However, many of us have experienced situations in which e-mail has been deliberately used to incite controversy and negative public opinion among school staff members.

A reasonable first step in such situations is to personally approach the individuals who are responsible for such e-mails to explain the impact of the behavior on themselves, on their colleagues, and on the school as a whole. Remind them of your school's policy or norms regarding e-mail use and—if you have the formal authority—be clear on the possible consequences of their actions. Many a colleague has come to me complaining about receiving an all-school e-mail that went to all faculty members when "everyone knows" that there were only one or two colleagues who personally needed to be spoken to. Approaching the individual is the right thing to do. If you then want to send an e-mail reiterating what the norms are and publicly announce the reason and decision that this line of e-mails needs come to a close, it can be an appropriate end to the discussion.

E-mails allow us to speak in ways we might not feel comfortable with if we were face to face. We might feel exempt from common courtesy and the norms of professionalism we use in our communities. Many educational technology organizations have resources for schools to use to describe what can and cannot be put in an e-mail. Use these tools to try to help you stay one step ahead of the possible difficult moments due to the increased use of technology. Expect to hear much debate on the challenges of professional communication in an age of "instant message" for decades to come.

What if the Hard Conversation Is a Needed Apology?

Often times, saying "I'm sorry" is the hardest conversation to have. We fear that we will lose face or be humiliated. Most of these concerns are about our own comfort, not about dealing with the impact of our behavior. To restore the other person's dignity and show the offended party that you are sorry and want to repair the relationship, Aaron Lazare (2004) has five steps to creating an apology that works.

- Correctly identify the party or parties to whom you owe an apology.
- Acknowledge the offending behavior in adequate detail.
- Recognize the impact the behavior had on the victim.
- Confirm that the grievance violated a social or moral contract by showing shame, remorse, humility, sincerity, and a wish to reclaim trust.
- Make reparations. Offer to do something, change something.

Consider this sample apology:

Maria, I am sorry for cutting you off in our meeting today. I snapped at you and didn't allow you to continue with your idea. My behavior was belittling and disrespectful. All the explanation in the world for my responses today and my reasons for acting inappropriately don't matter. What matters is that I messed up, I feel bad about my actions toward you, and I will try not do so again. I am sorry.

Don't do the following in your apology. Try to avoid "derailing" the apology, as Lazare describes it, by

- offering a vague and incomplete acknowledgement
  (saying, "I am sorry" with no more explanation);
- using an impersonal or passive voice; not owning the mistake
  (saying, "Mistakes were made," but not putting them in a first person, active verb);
- making the offense conditional; let go of any "ifs"
  (saying, "If mistakes were made, then I am sorry");
- implying that the victim might be damaged or weak
  (saying, "If anyone was hurt" or "If you were offended . . .");
- minimizing the offense
  (saying, "In the scheme of things, we have done a good job. Your complaint is one of so few. . . .");
- using the empathic "I am sorry" that denies your responsibility
  (saying, "I am sorry you suffered so much damage," or "I am sorry you are upset with me");
- apologizing in general, to a group, rather than to the victim
  (saying, "You all know how sorry I am");
- apologizing for the wrong offense
  (saying, "I'm sorry for the embarrassment I caused the school").

An old gospel song says, "I'm gonna clean up what I messed up and start all over again." To make your relationship with someone stronger and healthier, an apology can be the best hard conversation you could have.

This district office professional developer shares a story in which she found her relationship with a colleague much improved after she admitted her mistake.

If I have an opinion, I pretty much tell you how I feel. I remember going into a meeting with a group of about 12 people, and while I knew most folks in the room, I didn't know everyone there very well. We were going to work together on a project for the next year or so, we began by sharing stories in order to do a "get to know you" activity.

We all went around and began telling our stories and without thinking, I ended up telling a story that mocked a certain population of people. After the meeting ended, my close friend in the group came up to me to tell me that the woman right next to me was a member of that group—a very active and strong member. I put my foot in my mouth big time. I sat with this embarrassment all weekend and through half of one more meeting. It was awful.

I finally went up to her and said, "I am sorry for having made fun of your group. It was completely uncalled for. It was unacceptable and it won't happen again. I apologize."

My colleague was beyond gracious. She accepted my apology and smiled, and we giggled a bit together. I have never forgotten her kindness.

What if It Is Hard for Me to Praise?

Some of us find saying "Good job" truly uncomfortable. But praising someone with specificity and sincerity can be one of the best adult-to-adult communication skills you can learn.

The Los Angeles County Office of Education (2002) has a four-step method for praising with intention and finesse.

Step 1: Describe the behavior or accomplishment being praised.

Step 2: Give the person the reason why the behavior or accomplishment is being praised.

Step 3: Provide a positive consequence for the behavior or accomplishment.

Step 4: Request acknowledgement from the person indicating that he or she understands why he or she is being praised.

Praise should have the following characteristics:

- Immediately follow the accomplishment
- Be specific to the accomplishment
- Be natural rather than theatrical
- Be private most of the time
- Be individualized
- Be attributed to effort and ability

Here is an example of planned and intentional praise:

Kathy, thank you for your skillful facilitation of the meeting today, especially the way your framing of the situation made it easy for us to see the problem in a new light. Using the word "opportunity" versus "crisis" made all the difference. Please know that your facilitation had a truly positive impact on how everything went. Thank you.

It's never to late to learn this important skill, as this veteran principal found out from his staff.

I am not a man who is prone to praise. A wink or a smile or a pat on the shoulder is about as complimentary as I get. I find the touchy-feely part of this management work is just not me. I know you need to applaud folks for a good job and not just in a sarcastic way, like "Hey, that was an adequate presentation. Laugh laugh." So I am working on being more specific and actually writing an e-mail or giving a verbal thank you to one of my classified staff about the great work they are doing, and I am putting in the extra two sentences of details.

I think I sound clumsy, but my staff really thanks me for the recognition. I find it somewhat shocking, actually. They really appreciate being noticed and complimented. I am a bit ill at ease doing it, like a rookie, but I know it works.

TIPS FOR EASIER COMMUNICATION

Everyone from your grandmother to your guru has tips for how to communicate more effectively. These tips are drawn from *Words That Hurt, Words That Heal,* by Joseph Telushkin (1996), and "Management Shorts," by organizational development consultant Andrea Corney (2004).

- Say "thank you" more often. Show appreciation and care for your colleagues. Do it formally and informally so they know you see them doing things well.
- Ask "How are you?" Know what is going on so you will be more able to support your colleagues when they need it and not have the hard conversation after something didn't get done.
- Ask "What do you need?" Show folks you are on their side and can help out.
- Don't gossip. Talk to the person directly. And try not to stick around when others begin to gossip.
- Ask for feedback on your own performance. Open the door for others to tell you their ideas and what works for them. Ask for feedback regularly to make it less of a big deal. If you get feedback, take responsibility for your part of the problem and act on the feedback you receive.
- Say "I don't know" when you really don't. Acknowledge that you are learning to do your job and you aren't perfect either. Looking human and admitting your own challenges makes it easier for others around you to deal with theirs.
- If someone needs to have a hard conversation with you, *listen.* Ask yourself, "Is there any validity in the criticism? Can I take what she has said and use it to improve myself?"

I spend a lot of time thinking about the hard psychological work it takes to be a professional and a leader, the need to be aware of your own assumptions, biases, values, and beliefs. I think about what we do to act on our beliefs—and what we don't do. I spend a lot of time in workshops on having conversations, watching individuals grapple with the truth that they *do* have the power to speak up around issues of professionalism and effective teaching and they *are* accountable to the students to do so.

Some participants avoid the work—it isn't "their job"; they aren't getting paid enough to do the hard stuff. Some are not fully aware of what they really want for the students with whom they work or the schools in which they work. As a coach and a trainer, I've helped people bring to the surface what is already there, what they already knew about how to be a more effective teacher and a more effective colleague. I've found that they were hungry for a reminder of their power and what they really can do.

Most people want to know how to say what hasn't been said. They aren't on a power trip. They aren't looking for a quick retort. They want to work in a place that is moving forward, takes risks, and is an exciting, vibrant, alive place to work where both teachers and kids thrive. These teachers want to take ownership of their schools, and they want to find their voice to make it happen. These tools are a way in.

SUMMARY

This chapter offered additional support for those who have difficulties talking to a supervisor, delivering praise, or making apologies. There are many other hard conversations that need to take place around issues within your own school culture, about curriculum choices, inequities of funding, meeting student needs or federal mandates. My hope is that you will use the tools in this book and, with some modifications, apply them to your specific situations to become more comfortable speaking up, no matter the topic.

9

Conclusion

*Authority is granted to people who are perceived as authoring their
own words, their own actions, their own lives, rather than playing a
scripted role at great remove from their own hearts.*

—Parker Palmer (1997)

This is what I know: Hard conversations are never *not* hard. They will,
for the most part, be awkward, uncomfortable, and require us to
participate in experiences we would rather avoid. Yet the discomfort we
might experience doesn't give us license to not have them.

I feel more mature when I can sit in the middle of a difficult situation
and withstand the discomfort. Something shifts in me and I feel grown
up—like the adult I know I can be. I feel more alive, more authentic. I
recognize my own ability to withstand something painful, and I grow
emotionally taller having been through the experience.

And even though I have become more adept at hard conversations, I
still depend on the tools that make up this book, following the Get
Clear—Craft—Communicate process.

GET CLEAR

Knowing Why I Hesitate

This involves learning more about myself and why I hesitate speaking up.
Whether it is my need to be liked or my concern that I am too judgmental, just
knowing that I have much in common with others and their fears helps me
know I am not alone in what stops me. We all must know what our "default
positions" are and not let those get in the way of moving forward.

Asking Myself the Right Questions at the Right Time

This skill requires being metacognitive and asking myself questions ahead of time; not doing the "Ready—FIRE" approach, but instead, being thoughtful, considering the do-ability of what I would like to see, determining the consequences if I don't speak up, and thinking through how emotional I am and what facts I need to gather so I can speak from a place of calm.

CRAFT

Finding the Professional Language

I must determine which words I can use most confidently so I sound as professional as possible. I must have clear expectations for teacher (or other professional) behavior, both inside and outside of the classroom that is recognized by everyone in the school as "what we do." Then the hard conversation comes from a set of articulated norms for professional actions. It isn't a conversation laden with fuzzy, subjective adjectives, but instead a dialogue about measurable and objective behaviors.

Making a Plan

Going through an outcome map, I become ever more fluent in my description not only of the behaviors that would be more effective, but also what I might do to support my colleague in doing them. By thinking through what might be stopping my colleagues from executing those behaviors, I gain an understanding of others and become more capable in providing assistance to them.

COMMUNICATE

Scripting My Initial Comments

It is easier for me to speak up knowing that I have my initial sentences written out and that they include an opening line that doesn't shut someone down immediately, knowing that I have professional language and specific examples of what is going on, and knowing that I have described the impact of that behavior on others in a manner that is professional and thoughtful.

Determining the *Whats, Wheres,* and *Whens*

Being intentional—about where I choose to talk to my colleague, when I choose to speak, and what I do with my voice and my body—assists me to communicate most effectively. Consciously deciding which environment would be best and which language would be most beneficial to getting my point across make it a less complicated conversation to engage in. All of these tools support me, along with coming back to my bigger vision for what it means to be professional educators and how we need to communicate with one another. If we look at the educational research and our own work in classrooms and schools to determine what it means to be an effective educator, then we must speak up when we don't see those actions taking place. We must talk to one another about our profession. We must "author" our own lives as professionals and not wait for others to tell us who to be. We must not muffle ourselves any longer, but find our voices for the sake of the students we serve.

WHERE TO NEXT?

The next logical place to go in this conversation about being more professional in our communications is away from the role of speaker in these hard conversations and to the role of the listener. What can we do in shaping our school communities so that we are not only able to thoughtfully articulate our professional judgment in an honest and authentic way, but we are also able to *listen* openly and not shut down when the going gets tough?

Our next steps need to include building our capacity to courageously listen when we are on the receiving end of a hard conversation. How do we sit with the discomfort and not become defensive or paralyzed? What can we do and say to stay engaged although we might be hurt? It is the work of *all* members of the professional community to develop the skills to work together in this way. It is a vision of how we can work together that is both scary and daring . . . and necessary.

As mentioned in the preface, Audre Lorde (1984) wrote, "While we wait in silence for that final luxury of fearlessness, the weight of that silence will choke us" (pp. 41–44). We cannot afford to stay quiet. And truthfully, we just don't have that kind of time. Our schools and our students need us now.

Resource A

Extended List of Professional Teacher Behaviors

CLASSROOM MANAGEMENT AND CLIMATE

- Does the teacher make clear the procedures that are needed to have a well-run classroom? If so, how? Do students seem to know what to do
  - when they sit down (bell work),
  - when they hand in a paper,
  - when they are done working,
  - when they move around the room, and
  - when they move into groups?
- How does the teacher greet the students and begin the class session? How does the teacher build community at the start of the lesson? Does the teacher check in after the weekend or holidays?
- Do you hear the students asking questions about the process they are using? If so, how? Has the teacher put the directions or procedures in writing as well as stating them verbally?
- When doing transitions, how does the teacher move students effectively and efficiently from floor to desk or have students move into groups? What types of directions are given?
- Does the teacher model procedures, such as how to line up correctly or how to take a test?
- Is the teacher mindful from where she is teaching? Does she move around the room instructing from the place that will most benefit student learning?
- Does the teacher place an agenda on the board or is there a schedule up so students know what is coming?
- Does the teacher have a ritual so it is easy for students to understand what to do when they come into the room for the class or after recess? Do they have a way of ending the day or the class?
- Does the teacher have a discipline plan and is he consistent with it? Has it been reviewed and do students know the consequences of certain actions?

- Does the teacher keep track of time? If so, how? Does she verbally announce times for processing activities in order to keep students moving at an appropriate pace? Does she check in to see whether students need more time?
- Does the teacher have equipment and materials logically located? If so, how? Can the students get to the garbage can or wire baskets or locations in the room to pick up materials? Can they see the notes on the board? Can the teacher get to everyone and monitor easily?
- Does the teacher move the students around effectively to support the instruction? If so, how? Do students move easily from group to lecture to partner processing?
- Does the teacher work with the classroom aides in the room? If so, how? Are the aides able to sit near the students they work with or find space to sit?
- Does it appear on a syllabus or on the walls that agreements are made with regard to listening to each other, self-management, and so forth? If so, how?
- How does the teacher attract the attention of the class before starting instruction? Does the teacher have signals for moments like this? If so, what are they, and are they effective?
- Does the teacher end the class or does the bell end the class? Does the teacher seem in control of the time as the bell rings? If so, how?
- If you witness a student saying something disrespectful or derogatory, do you notice the teacher dealing with the student and the comment in a way that makes the class feel safe? If so, how?
- Does the teacher know when certain students might be confused and is he proactive about addressing the misconception in a way that doesn't allow the whole group to derail the lesson due to frustration?
- When you walk in the room, do you hear the students talking and working or do you hear the teacher? For how long? Is it the same students talking one by one or do all students get an opportunity to process the material?
- When you hear the students talking, is it asking about how to do something with the content or is it about the content itself? Do the students steer and shape the conversation about the content, helping themselves progress?
- Do you see covert and overt active participation of all students? If so, how?
- Do you see the teacher use wait time deliberately so more students get a chance to think about the question? If so, how?
- Does the teacher smile or laugh? Does the teacher have eye contact with students (if culturally appropriate)?
- Is the teacher aware of tone and body language and use an approachable and a credible voice in the right situations?
- Does the teacher appear comfortable in the presence of all students? If so, how?

- Does the teacher appear to like all students? Does she show favorites? Do you hear positive comments for some students and not for others?
- Does the teacher listen to all students? Does he interrupt students or certain groups of students?
- What is on the walls of the room? Are they distracting or over- or understimulating? Are the messages the walls send positive and do they engage students?
- Does the teacher have student work up on the walls? If so, is there something up from all students? If so, is it clear that it isn't graded work or evaluated in some way?
- How does the teacher redirect students who are off task? Is it done in a respectful manner, for example, cuing students nonverbally? If so, how?
- What happens when a student makes a mistake? How does the teacher respond? What is the climate like with regard to risk taking and sharing in whole group moments? Does the teacher acknowledge her mistakes as well? If so, how?
- Does the teacher articulate that there are a variety of ways of what it means to be smart, not just knowing content well?
- Does the teacher acknowledge feelings of students along with teaching content? If so, how? Does he state this acknowledgment in a respectful manner versus being patronizing (e.g., "I know some of you are nervous about this test . . ." versus "You shouldn't be freaked out. If you had studied. . . .")?
- Does the teacher stop and address homophobic, racist, or sexist and other judgmental or bullying comments (physical appearance or disability) and do so in a way that makes it clear that those types of comments are not to be said again in the classroom and then explain why? Is she consistent with this message through what is on the walls and what is said?
- Does the teacher model courteous behavior and good citizenship? If so, how?

MEETING THE NEEDS OF A VARIETY OF LEARNERS

- Does the teacher strive to learn about the personalities and social backgrounds of her students? If so, how? Does the teacher talk with counselors, support staff, students themselves, and parents?
- Does the teacher know enough about the students to know which students can relate to certain material based on gender, culture, immigration status, or socioeconomic status? If so, how?
- Does the teacher show an understanding of strategies to support those students who need support through special education services? If so, how?

- Is the teacher aware of who in his classroom is an English language learner (ELL) and who speaks another language as his or her primary language?
- Does the teacher show an understanding of ELL strategies in order to engage ELL students effectively? Does the teacher offer additional supports or use specially designed academic instruction in English (SDAIE) strategies? Do ELL students feel engaged and safe in the classroom? If so, how?
- Does the teacher allow opportunities for ELL students to speak in their primary language in order to understand the course content? Do students feel safe speaking no matter the language they use?
- Does the teacher know the students and the school cultures well enough to be able to add examples and illustrations that will connect to the students' lives? If so, how?
- Does the teacher feel comfortable acknowledging and soliciting students' experiences and histories when appropriate to the classroom discussion and content?
- Does the teacher pick up on day-to-day "messages" from students? Is she attentive to revealing messages in classroom work or responses? If so, how?
- Does the teacher show respect for all students? If so, how? Does he speak to them courteously, acknowledging their opinions and values, even if they are different from the teacher's opinion?
- Does the teacher use language that validates and respects all home cultures and family structures?
- Does the teacher provide opportunities for *all* students to learn, process, share, and participate, not just those who have their hands up? If so, how? And when students do participate, does the teacher listen and look at all students?
- Does the teacher seem to positively presuppose that all kids can learn and achieve in her classroom? If so, how? Does she speak to the potential of students and presuppose they can do the work or does she speak to their deficits or their inability to accomplish a task?
- Does the teacher recognize his role goes beyond the teaching of content to the teaching of students? If so, how? Does this teaching include how to learn, how to live, and how to be with others?
- Does the teacher provide opportunities for students to discuss their lives, their hopes, and dreams for themselves? If so, how?
- Does the teacher understand how physical and emotional development at certain ages impacts student learning? Does she "understand" the middle schooler, the kindergartener, the senior? If so, how?
- Does the teacher feel he is a "text person" and does he take on the responsibility of being a role model for the students to "read"? If so, how?
- Is the teacher mindful of motivational techniques? Does she increase or decrease the level of concern to assist students to do the work at

hand (e.g., offering time limits, solo work, or no resources versus all the time in the world, a partner, and an open notebook)

PLANNING LESSONS AND INSTRUCTIONAL DELIVERY

- Does the teacher tell the students what they will be doing to show him that they understand the material in the lesson? If so, how? Does he put it on the board or verbalize it?
- Does the teacher have a syllabus that sets some long-range goals for students or have a unit cover sheet or a lesson plan book or set of benchmarks that she is working from?
- Does the teacher work with others at his grade level or in his course area to align with the timing and pacing of others and determine to cover essential key learning as a group?
- Does the teacher strive to create lessons and experiences for students that help them learn autonomy, choice, and how to deal with others? If so, how?
- Does the teacher know her objectives and is she able to differentiate the objectives by shifting the parts of an objective to accommodate for individual differences? If so, how?
- Does the teacher teach to what he is going to ultimately grade? If so, how? Is he able to articulate what students will need to know and be able to do on a given assignment and then teach those components and skills to the students so they will be successful?
- Does the teacher have a background in the subject area?
- Does the teacher continually expand her content knowledge by attending conferences, participating in collegial discussions about her course, and reading professional journals?
- Does the teacher know how to creatively adapt the textbook to meet the needs of her students? If so, how?
- Is the teacher aware of the big ideas and how and why they fit together? Can the teacher design lessons with these key ideas in such a way that students are successful? If so, how?
- Does the teacher know the state frameworks and the content and expectations of the given course, and can he design lessons that address both those needs? If so, how?
- Does the teacher integrate her subject matter with other disciplines when appropriate? If so, how?
- Does the teacher design lessons with adequate amounts of active participation in his class in order to facilitate learning for the students? If so, how?
- If and when the teacher lectures or offers direct instruction to the students, does the teacher plan active participation strategies that will allow her to monitor and assess the understanding of the students with regard to the subject? If so, how?

- Does the teacher use a variety of strategies to engage students? If so, how? Do these include videos, audio recordings, small group discussions, whole group discussions, manipulatives, photography, games, realia (such as maps, real life models, or objects), technology, and other resources?
- Does the teacher use technology effectively in his classes? Does he access Web resources, use PowerPoint, Smart Boards, Think Pads, and so forth?
- Does the teacher urge students to think critically and design lessons that require them to work at the higher levels of Bloom's taxonomy (application, analysis, synthesis, evaluation)? If so, how?
- Does the teacher physically write out a lesson plan or notes or slides for a given lesson?
- Does she stick to that lesson plan and if not, could she articulate her reasons for not moving forward with that specific plan?
- Is the teacher mindful of the objective at hand, and if students get him off topic does he bring the conversation back to the objective? If not, can the teacher explain why he decided to "birdwalk"?
- Does the teacher use an anticipatory set to bring forward the students' prior knowledge and connect them to the current learning?
- Is the teacher aware of how long a given activity will take and make adjustments based on the level of understanding the group has?
- Does the teacher plan for smooth transitions between activities?
- Does the teacher instruct using wait time and the phrase, "Everybody think . . ." instead of saying, "Who can tell me . . . ?" and only having one student at a time responding?
- Does the teacher model for the students whatever process or format the students will need to use? If so, how? Does the teacher show sample papers, go through an example of an assignment, or do a demonstration of the lab before the students are required to do it independently?
- When you hear the teacher providing instruction, do you hear specific examples being given? If so, how? Does the teacher reference connections that seem to make sense to the students?
- Does the teacher allow for accommodations so that in a given assignment students are offered options or a change of conditions? If so, how?
- Does the teacher attempt to use all the modalities, visual, aural, and kinesthetic? Does she work outside her comfort zone to meet these needs? If so, how?
- Does the teacher use a combination of competition, individual performance, and collaborative teamwork in his active participation strategies? If so, how?
- Does the teacher teach cooperative learning strategies, especially if she is grading a student on specific group work behaviors or having a student peer assess?
- Does the teacher offer relevant and novel assignments that engage students in applying their knowledge in a way that is meaningful for them? If so, how?

- Does the teacher not only teach knowledge about the subject but also teach the knowledge arts—the skills required to work in the given subject? If so, how?
- Does the teacher help the students learn problem-solving strategies? If so, how?
- Does the teacher help students see the connections of their learning to real life situations? If so, how?
- Does the teacher pace the lesson to allow for review, synthesis, or closure of the lesson?

ASSESSMENT

- Does the teacher help the student become more self-directed, self-monitoring and self-modifying? If so, how? Does he help student self-review and set goals?
- Do you see the teacher walking around the room to check on student progress?
- Is the teacher able to gauge students' progress and, if asked, able to do a quick analysis of how the student is doing in class, possibly without a look at the grade book?
- Does the teacher provide one-on-one feedback to the students at that time or does she come back to the front to give an "I saw a lot of" so students know how they are doing? If so, how?
- Does the teacher have rubrics, clear assignment sheets, and clear directions? Are the assignments posted as well as offered to the students?
- Does the teacher have a wide variety of formative assessments in the classroom?
- Can the teacher articulate to you how and why he weights his grades a certain way?
- Does the teacher allow for makeup work or retaking of exams and tests? If so, what is his process and grading standard for those redos?
- When designing assignments, is the teacher aware of structural barriers (e.g., no computer at home, difficulty in finding someone to interview, etc.) that might limit some students from doing the work?
- Does the teacher have a grade reporting system that she uses? If so, how does it work?
- Does the teacher accept incomplete or late work? How frequently? What procedures are in place to collect the work?
- Does he share updates on grades and current progress so students are aware of how they are doing? If so, how?
- Does the teacher have in place a self-assessment system that helps students identify learning goals and use the information to improve their achievement?
- Does the teacher have an evaluation system that allows for feedback around effort and not just academic competency?

- Does the teacher use a wide variety of appropriate assessments? If looking at the grade book, could you see projects, journals, tests, and essays in a mix versus one type of grade only?
- Do you hear the teacher giving feedback to students in whole group and small group instruction? If so, how? Is the feedback positive and specific?
- Does the teacher have the students check work with each other and does she have a process for doing so?
- Does the teacher ask the students to keep track of their own assignments? If so, how?
- Does the teacher communicate responsively with parents in a timely fashion, such as answering calls, meeting with parents, or showing up to back-to-school night? If so, how?

DEVELOPING AS A PROFESSIONAL EDUCATOR

- Does the teacher attend workshops, afternoon sessions, weekend retreats, staff development days, and collaborative/grade level planning sessions? If so, which ones, and why?
- Does the teacher read journals, subject-specific books, and professional reading? Does she have "teacher books" on her desk? Does she make use of what is in the principal's office, on the instructional supervisor's desk, in the staff library, and in the professional development library? If so, can she explain her choices of reading?
- Does the teacher read articles sent around the school or put in his box for review?
- Does the teacher go to the staff lounge or the main office or the grade level areas? Does she talk to colleagues about teaching techniques or ask for ideas or support? If so, how?
- Does the teacher have a sense of what he wants to learn and take proactive steps to have that learning take place? Does he ask for professional development funds, plan to observe peers, and ask for a substitute to allow for professional learning time?
- Is the teacher aware of her teaching philosophy (content deliverer, social-emotional development of students, democratic society skills, career skills, etc.) and the strengths and limitations of that specific frame?
- Is the teacher willing to stretch to support and include teaching experiences and student opportunities that are outside what the teacher might feel should be taught?
- Does the teacher apply knowledge gained from these experiences into her teaching? If so, how? Do you see evidence of school- or districtwide initiative content or skills applied in her teaching?
- Does the teacher consistently reflect and analyze his teaching?
- When she reflects on a class, does it result in an adjustment to practice on her end? If so, how? Can she see what the "takeaways" are and what she might change for the next class session given the learning?

- When the teacher reflects on his instruction, does the tone seem blaming of kids and their abilities ("They can't do it") or less defensive and more self-aware ("I don't think I was clear enough with them here and here")?
- Is the teacher capable of articulating her strengths? If so, how? Which content areas are strong? What instructional techniques does she do well? And does she know her gaps and her biases, and how does she manage those weaknesses?
- Is the teacher self-managing, self-monitoring, and self-modifying? If so, how?
- Can the teacher draw from his prior knowledge and data to refine his instruction?
- Does she display a sense of resourcefulness and humor as she adjusts her instruction? If so, how? Or is it just "another thing I need to do now because of THIS year's class," or "just another initiative from the district . . ."?
- Does the teacher seek the perspectives of others and innovative ideas? If so, how? Do you hear the teacher say, "What do you think of . . .?" or "Do you have an idea for . . .?"
- When offered a suggestion for change, does the teacher use a "Yeah, but" response or does he "take it in" and think about its application in the classroom?
- When offered a suggestion that isn't clear enough to the teacher, does she ask for more clarification so it can be implemented? If so, how? Does she ask for support from others to try it?
- When offered a suggestion, does the teacher willingly try it and share results with colleagues?
- Does the teacher hold himself to a high standard for what he does and produces? If so, how?
- Does the teacher continually refine lessons and units and work to improve her teaching? If so, how?
- Is the teacher able to stand outside himself and see how he might be impacting others or be seen by others? If so, how?
- If the teacher is given feedback, does she listen to it and react appropriately, changing behavior if necessary? If so, how?
- Is the teacher open to rational *and* intuitive ways of thinking? If so, how?
- Is the teacher open to doing things in a way other than his way?
- Is the teacher open to hearing all perspectives? If so, how? And when hearing all perspectives, does she honor them or shut down?

PARTICIPATION IN SCHOOL COMMUNITY

- Does the teacher "show up"? Show up on time or late? Does she show up at staff meetings, department meetings, on staff development days, and at team meetings? Does the teacher show up at events that are related to school improvement?

- Does the teacher know, understand, respect, and follow the learning outcomes and course descriptions of his classes? If so, how? Does he follow the objectives for the department and the goals of the school?
- If asked to complete some paperwork or attend a meeting on behalf of the department or do some work for the team, does it get done?
- Does the teacher share an enthusiasm for the "pursuit of teaching excellence"? If so, how?
- Does the teacher look like she enjoys teaching, enjoys the school, and enjoys her colleagues? If so, how?
- Is the teacher aware of the school values, norms, and the way the school sees itself? Does the teacher work well within those values? If so, how? Does he embody them or just give them lip service?
- Does the teacher seem to understand the implicit or explicit code of dress for the teachers and other professionals in the school and wear appropriate clothing for the age of the students and the school culture? If so, how?
- Does the teacher hone her communication and process skills as well as work on her classroom instruction? If so, how?
- Does the teacher show consideration for the feelings of others? Say "Hello," say "Thank you," say "I'm sorry," say "What can I do to help?"
- Does the teacher gossip? Does he talk poorly of colleagues in your presence or to students?
- Is the teacher aware of her assumptions and values and know when they are getting in the way of moving forward with her colleagues, parents, and the school community?
- Does the teacher cooperate with special education staff so that services are provided to the students? Does she fill out the progress reports and do the required or suggested accommodations with a positive attitude?
- Does he work with counselors or administrators when there is a problem? Does he attend student study teams and do so in a "willing" way?
- Does the teacher manage her anxiety in a way that is appropriate, such as not yelling at staff or students?
- Does the teacher know of the hierarchy of positions in the school? Does he go to the appropriate person for the appropriate concern? Does the teacher go to someone at all and look for solutions rather than sit with the problem?
- Does the teacher want to work in a group and shows that by body language, contributions, and attitude? Does she seek to understand the other's point of view?
- When communicating with other adults, does the teacher ask for other perspectives?
- Does the person show an ability to listen for understanding and empathy?
- Does the teacher manage impulsivity or interrupt more often, inserting his point of view?

- Does the teacher use positive presuppositions when coming together with a group?
- Does the teacher seem to have a sense of humor? Can she laugh at herself?
- Is the teacher aware that he is not allowing equitable participation by talking too much at meetings or talking too little and not contributing?
- Does the teacher have a sense of personal space, body language, and appropriate sense of decorum in a given setting?

Resource B

School Savvy Etiquette

E-MAIL

Respectful Response

- Try to return e-mail within 48 hours.
- If you cannot get an e-mail response back in that time, send a courtesy e-mail stating you received the e-mail and when you can respond.
- If someone from the district office sends you something, either via e-mail or snail mail, please respond to it as soon as possible. In fact, respond to anyone at your site as soon as possible, too.
- Beware of "reply all"—know to whom the e-mail is going.
- Be aware of text messages as well. Anything in writing can be subpoenaed.
- If you have a strong feeling about the e-mail you have just received and you need to respond, use the following suggestions:
  o Wait 24 hours.
  o Draft a response in Word.
  o Send the draft to the department chair, your coach, or a colleague to read it for tone.
  o Cut and paste a final version into your response e-mail.
  o "cc:" your supervisor if you feel he or she needs to be "in the know."

Form

- Proof your writing to catch typos, mistaken or missing words, and grammatical errors.
- Use clear subject lines. Do *not* put names, especially *student names*, in the header. If you receive an e-mail with a student's name in the subject, change it to "Your student" before you send it back.
- Consider your use of capital letters—they can be perceived as hostile.

- Consider your opener—the reader might forget what a "yes" or "no" refers to. Begin with a greeting and a reiteration of the question or topic: "Hello . . . nice to hear from you . . . with regard to your invitation/concern/assignment . . ."
- Consider if e-mail is the correct medium for the topic. If you have gone back and forth two to three times, voice or face to face might be a better way of handling the situation.
- Less is more. Shorter is almost always better in e-mail exchange. Think Hemingway: short noun-verb sentences and bullets.
- Limit the number of different questions or issues in one e-mail. If you include too many, some may not get addressed in response, and that can irritate. If you do have several answers, state you will respond to the questions with responses directly below the question. If possible, put them in another color so your reader can easily see them.
- Be aware that e-mail can be subpoenaed in a court case. Write only what you'd want to be seen in that type of situation.

STAFF, DEPARTMENT, OR COLLABORATION MEETINGS

- Be on time to all meetings; in fact, be there a few minutes early.
- Bring what you need for the meeting. If they asked you to bring suggestions, paperwork filled out, or a set of something, do so.
- Consider your use of a computer during the meeting and whether it is supporting the work or getting in the way of real dialogue.
- Do not text message during the meeting.
- Be considerate and put your cell phone on vibrate. If you need to answer it, do so with a quick "Just a minute" and wait until you are out of the room to continue the conversation. Do not talk from the table to the door.
- Do not do crossword puzzles, read the newspaper, grade papers, or do lesson planning during the meeting—behave in a way you would want colleagues to attend at a meeting you were leading—full attention makes for a better result. It will get noticed if you don't.
- If a disgruntled colleague engages you, try to shift away from that energy. Don't continue whispering to them during the meeting.
- If you need to leave the meeting, try to let the administrator know ahead of time so that when you leave, it is expected.
- Avoid defensive reactions—eye rolling, sighing, shouting out, or giggling.
- Offer an apology if disrespectful.
- Explain yourself and your mood (if stressed or if angry).
- If you are running the meeting, have an agenda and facilitate well. Learn how to keep things on track, how to ask people to adhere to norms, and how to work effectively with conflict.

WORKING WITH OFFICE AND SUPPORT STAFF

- Do not treat them as your assistants or with a condescending tone.
- Say hello to them when you come into the office and use eye contact.
- Ask if it is a good time to review something you need or when that time would be.
- If requesting an item, something copied, something done, give explicit instructions for the task. Don't assume understanding.
- Be aware of the procedures in place. If copying is done at 9 a.m., have it ready by then.
- Be aware of the proper channels. Do you need to get approval by a supervisor or a front office administrator to have a support staff assist you with something?
- Consider priorities; that is, what is immediate (something unsanitary on the floor that needs to be swept up immediately) versus something that can wait (fixing a light).
- If you break something or finish with something, please let someone know so they can handle it.
- Acknowledge everything they do for you and thank them.
- If something is not done, or a mistake has been made, address it directly, but in an understanding, unthreatening way.

DRESS

- Ask directly if there is a dress code for teachers.
- Read the student dress code and, by all means, do not break it.
- Make a visual poll of what your colleagues are wearing and go for a middle ground.

CONFLICT

- If you are struggling with something or someone, talk it through with your coach, the new teacher mentor at your school, or a very trusted colleague. Do not tell everyone in the lunchroom. Do not tell the parents about it when they come to pick up their children.
- If you are going into a difficult meeting with your supervisor or the principal, bring your coach or a trusted colleague if you can.
- If you can, go to the source whenever possible.
- Do not shout across the hallways or the quad to the person; approach him or her face-to-face.
- Do not send notes or e-mails stating only, "How about returning this?" or "How about getting this done?" and then adding an attachment. The impression isn't a good one.
- Do not have the difficult discussion in front of students.
- Do not talk to students about your conflicts with others.

- When discussing events, try to go "global/general" versus name dropping.
- Exercise care and caution regarding the time and place for addressing delicate topics, such as before school, after school, or during passing periods. Think about the impact.

ADDITIONAL SCHOOL SAVVY TOPICS FOR DISCUSSION

- *Relationships and Communication With All Support Staff*
  - Custodians, Aides, Volunteers
- *Technology*
  - Being on Friendster, MySpace, Facebook, or other Web-based service where you have a personal site and your pictures up so your students and their parents can see
- *Boundaries with Students*
  - Talking about students in front of other students
  - Talking with them appropriately in the hallways or on the campus
  - Talking to students about other teachers
  - Talking to students when they are disrespectful of other teachers
- *Boundaries with Colleagues and Parents*
  - Talking in the bathroom, in the parking lot, in the lunchroom
  - Talking in the grocery store, at a party, in the community
- *Classroom Sharing*
  - Materials, space, cleanliness
- *Curriculum and Materials*
  - Rewinding movies
  - Returning equipment (video cameras, calculators)
  - Using someone's personal property
  - Textbook sharing
  - Keeping things organized
- *Absences*
  - Leaving clear substitute plans
  - Expectations of others covering classes for you
  - Personal days, sick days—How many? How often?
- *Thinking Aloud in Front of Certain Audiences*
  - Who is your ally? Your critical friend?
  - To whom can you vent? Cry in front of? To whom can't you vent?
  - Considering political beliefs—being tolerant of others' point of view
- *Family and Pets*
  - Bringing your dog, parrot, or infant or child to work
  - Bringing them to meetings or professional development
  - What is legal? What is appropriate?
- *Taking a Leave or Being Released*
  - Sharing info about a leave/pregnancy/change-of-employment status
  - How to talk about it, with whom, and when

- *Categories for Which One Needs Interpersonal and School Savviness*
  - o Time—What is late?
  - o Keeping your word
  - o Sharing personal info in a professional space
  - o Emotional expression boundaries: Can you cry? Yell?
  - o Manners/courtesy
  - o Noise levels—What is loud? Space—too close?
  - o Dress—What is appropriate?
  - o Food—Sharing it? Bringing it?
  - o Language use—Is slang or swearing OK?
  - o Hygiene

Resource C

Additional Sample Scripts Step by Step

SET THE TONE AND PURPOSE OF THE CONVERSATION

- Jill, I want to talk to you about something you said yesterday at the meeting. I know your intentions were earnest, but since the impact was something I don't think you meant, we need to clear this up now before we move into the next discussion.
- Steve, something has been sitting with me all weekend, and I realize that I cannot move forward with you on this project unless I clear it up. It is important to me that I put this on the table because I want us to be able to work effectively together.
- Abby, your management style and organization have really been supportive to so many students this year as they transition into high school, and there is another aspect to teaching that I think you need to refine in order to support even more students in your classroom.
- Scott, you know your subject well and your understanding of physics is admirable. We need to talk about how you can get that understanding across to even more students than you already do.

GET TO THE POINT AND NAME IT PROFESSIONALLY

- It is about meeting the needs of all learners.
- It has to do with your participation in the work group.
- It has to do with engaging the students and helping them be more enthusiastic about the content of the class.
- We need to talk about how you can get that understanding across to even more students than you already do through incorporating more active instructional strategies and monitoring into your lessons.

GIVE SPECIFIC EXAMPLES

- Your comment about the students from High Point Elementary not being "ready for prime time" showed a disrespect toward them and your colleagues that worked with them, and while you did say you would provide some interventions for those students to bring them on board, the comment left others feeling insulted.
- Your getting up and taking phone calls twice during our meeting was incredibly distracting to me.
- I have noticed in the last two observations that you start the class by asking everyone to look at the white board for the warm-up and then when they are done, you move directly into the subject for the day. I have also noticed in the last hour I watched that although it was clear that students, especially Trudy, had a lot to say about their personal connection with the material, you said, "We need to get through the notes."
- I noticed in my observation today that you lectured for 45 of the 60 minutes and that you called on only those students who raised their hands. It turned out that over 50% of your class didn't participate in class today. This is a pattern I have seen in my other two observations as well.

DESCRIBE THE EFFECT OF THIS BEHAVIOR ON THE SCHOOL, COLLEAGUES, OR STUDENTS

- We can't all move together as a district working group if a certain segment is feeling put down.
- I felt it showed a disregard for the work of the group as if you discounted our time together and felt phone calls were more important. I, for one, don't feel as willing to put in much work when your leaving says to me you don't feel it is an important endeavor.
- By not offering a personal greeting to students at the beginning of class and discounting Trudy's stories, you aren't creating as safe an environment as you could where you and the students can bring personal aspects of themselves.
- This lack of active participation strategies doesn't work when the students are the ones that need to demonstrate understanding of the material.

SHARE YOUR WILLINGNESS TO RESOLVE THE ISSUE AND HAVE A DIALOGUE AND DISCUSSION

- It would be best if you didn't use that comment or others like it as we talk about other schools. Does that make sense?

- Is there some way we could have you turn off the phone during the meeting or make some arrangements so it doesn't distract us? What might work?
- I know students would feel better if they were able to share and be heard by you. How do you see this situation? How can we look at it together?
- This is a critical issue in the classroom and one we need to deal with now. What are your immediate thoughts?

THE ANNOTATED SCRIPTS IN THEIR ENTIRETY

- Jill, I want to talk to you about something you said yesterday at the meeting. I know your intentions were well-meaning, but since the impact was something I don't think you meant, I need to tell you about it now before we move into the next discussion (SETTING THE TONE). It was about meeting the needs of all learners (NAMING THE ISSUE). Your comment about the students from High Point Elementary not being "ready for prime time" showed a disrespect towards the students and your colleagues who worked with them (GIVING SPECIFIC EXAMPLES) and, while you did say you would provide some interventions for those students to bring them on board, the comment left others feeling insulted. We can't all move together as a district working group if a certain segment is feeling put down (DESCRIBING THE IMPACT). It would be best if you didn't use that comment or others like it as we talk about other schools. Does that make sense? Can you see this from their perspective? (INDICATING A WISH TO DIALOGUE.)
- Steve, something has been sitting with me all weekend and I realize that I cannot move forward with you on this project unless I talk to you about it. It is important to me that I put this on the table because I want us to be able to work effectively together (SETTING THE TONE). It has to do with your participation in the work group (NAMING THE ISSUE). Your getting up and taking phone calls twice during our meeting was incredibly distracting to me (GIVING SPECIFIC EXAMPLE). I felt it showed a disregard for the work of the group as if you discounted our time together and felt phone calls were more important. I, for one, don't feel as willing to put in much work when your leaving says to me you don't feel it is an important endeavor (DESCRIBING THE IMPACT). Is there some way we could have you turn off the phone during the meeting or make some arrangements so it doesn't distract us? What might work? (INDICATING A WISH TO DIALOGUE.)
- Abby, your management style and organization have really been supportive to so many students this year as they transition into high school, and there is another aspect to teaching that I think you need to refine in order to support even more students in your classroom (SETTING THE TONE). It has to do with engaging the students and helping them be more enthusiastic about the content of the class

(NAMING THE ISSUE). I have noticed in the last two observations that you start the class by asking everyone to look at the white board for the warm-up, and then when they are done, you move directly into the subject for the day. I have also noticed in the last hour I watched that although it was clear that students, especially Trudy, had a lot to say about their personal connection with the material, you said, "We need to get through the notes" (GIVING SPECIFIC EXAMPLE). By not offering a personal greeting to students at the beginning of class and discounting Trudy's stories, you aren't creating as safe an environment as you could where you and the students can bring personal aspects of themselves (DESCRIBING THE IMPACT). How do you see this situation? How can we look at it together? (INDICATING WISH FOR DIALOGUE.)

- Scott, you know your subject well and your understanding of physics is admirable (SETTING THE TONE). We need to talk about how you can get that understanding across to even more students than you already do through incorporating more active instructional strategies and monitoring into your lessons (NAMING THE ISSUE). I noticed in my observation today that you lectured for 45 of the 60 minutes and that you called on only those students who raised their hands. It turned out that over 50% of your class didn't participate in class today. This is a pattern I have seen in my other two observations as well (GIVING SPECIFIC EXAMPLES). Students are not being provided structured opportunities to process the material in class, and this lack of active participation strategies doesn't work when the students are the ones that need to demonstrate understanding of the material (DESCRIBING THE IMPACT). This is a critical issue in the classroom and one we need to deal with now. What are your immediate thoughts? (INDICATING A WISH TO DIALOGUE.)

References and Suggested Readings

Abrams, J. (2001). A new way of thinking: Beginning teacher coaching through Garmston's and Costa's states of mind. *English Leadership Quarterly, 24*(1), pp. 2–4.

Abrams, J. (2003). Having hard conversations. *Utah Special Educator, 24*(2), pp. 14–15.

Arbinger Institute. (2000). *Leadership and self-deception: Getting out of the box.* San Francisco: Berrett-Koehler.

Bodaken, B., & Fritz, R. (2006). *The managerial moment of truth: The essential step in helping people improve performance.* New York: Free Press.

Brandon, R., & Seldman, M. (2004). *Survival of the savvy: High-integrity political tactics for career and company success.* New York: Free Press.

Bryk, A., & Schneider, B. (2002). *Trust in schools: A core resource for improvement.* New York: Russell Sage.

Checkley, K., & Kelly, L. (1999). Toward better teacher education: A conversation with Asa Hilliard. *Educational Leadership, 56*(8), 58–62.

Corney, A. (2004). *Management shorts #17: Feedback basics.* Retrieved September 20, 2008 from http://www.acorn-od.com/shorts/archive/shorts-17.html.

Corney, A. (2004). *Management shorts#19: Getting useful feedback.* Retrieved September 20, 2008 from http://www.acorn-od.com/shorts/archive/shorts-19.html.

Costa A. L., & Garmston, R. (2002). *Cognitive coaching: A foundation for renaissance schools* (2nd ed.). Norwood, MA: Christopher-Gordon.

Costa, A. L., & Kallick, B. (2004). *Assessment strategies for self-directed learning.* Thousand Oaks, CA: Corwin Press.

Covey, S. (2006). *The speed of trust: The one thing that changes everything.* New York: Free Press.

Crowley, K., & Elster, K. (2006). *Working with you is killing me: Freeing yourself from emotional traps at work.* New York: Warner Business Books.

Elgin, S. H. (1989). *Success with the gentle art of verbal self-defense.* Englewood Cliffs, NJ: Prentice Hall.

Fullan, M. (1990, March). Presented at the annual meeting of the Association for Supervision and Curriculum Development, San Diego, CA.

Garmston, R. J., & Wellman, B. (1999). *The adaptive school: A sourcebook for developing collaborative groups.* Norwood, MA: Christopher-Gordon.

Grinder, M. (2007). *The elusive obvious.* Battleground, WA: Michael Grinder and Associates.

Heifetz, R., Kania, J., & Kramer, M. (2004, Winter). Leading boldly. *Stanford Social Innovation Review,* pp. 21–31.

Kegan, R., & Lahey, L. L. (2001). *How the way we talk can change the way we work: Seven languages for transformation.* San Francisco: Jossey-Bass.

Lazare, A. (2004). *On apology.* New York: Oxford University Press.

Lee, E. (2002, February). *Putting race on the table.* Workshop presented at the New Teachers Center Symposium, Santa Cruz, CA.

Lerner, H. G. (2001). *The dance of connection: How to talk to someone when you're mad, hurt, scared, frustrated, insulted, betrayed, or desperate.* New York: HarperCollins.

Lipton, L., & Wellman, B. (with Humbard, C.). (2001). *Mentoring matters: A practical guide to learning-focused relationships.* Sherman, CT: MiraVia.

Lorde, A. (1984). *Sister outsider: Essays and speeches.* Berkeley, CA: Crossing Press.

Los Angeles County Office of Education. (2002). *Teacher expectations-student achievement: Coordinator manual.* Los Angeles: Author.

Meyerson, D. E. (2001). *Tempered radicals: How people use difference to inspire change at work.* Boston: Harvard Business School Press.

Palmer, P. J. (1997, November/December). The heart of a teacher: identity and integrity in teaching. *Change Magazine, 29*(6), pp. 14–21.

Palmer, P. J. (1998). *The courage to teach: Exploring the inner landscape of a teacher's life.* San Francisco: Jossey-Bass.

Palmer, P. J. (2004). *A hidden wholeness: The journey toward an undivided life.* San Francisco: Jossey-Bass.

Patterson, K., Grenny, J., McMillan, R., & Switzler, A. (2002). *Crucial conversations: Tools for talking when stakes are high.* New York: McGraw-Hill.

Patterson, K., Grenny, J., McMillan, R., & Switzler, A. (2005). *Crucial confrontations: Tools for resolving broken promises, violated expectations, and bad behavior.* New York: McGraw-Hill.

Pearce, T. (2000, April 30). Leadership coaching. A contact sport. *San Francisco Examiner.* Available at http://leading1.web.aplus.net/tp-art-coaching.html.

Perkins, D. (2002). *King Arthur's Round Table.* New York: Wiley.

Platt, A. D., Tripp, C. E., Ogden, W. R., & Fraser, R. G. (2000). *The skillful leader: Confronting mediocre teaching.* Acton, MA: Ready About Press.

Platt, A. D., Tripp, C. E., Fraser, R. G., Warnock, J. R., & Curtis, R. E. (2008). *The skillful leader II: Confronting conditions that undermine learning.* Acton, MA: Ready About Press.

Quate, S. (2004). Critical friends groups. In L. B. Easton (Ed.), *Powerful designs for professional learning* (pp. 95–102). Oxford, OH: National Staff Development Council.

Saphier, J. (1993). *How to make supervision and evaluation really work.* Acton, MA: Research for Better Teaching.

Scott, S. (2002). *Fierce conversations: Achieving success at work & in life, one conversation at a time.* New York: Viking Press.

Sizer, T. R. & Sizer, N. F. (1999). *The students are watching: Schools and the moral contract.* Boston: Beacon Press.

Sparks, D. (2005). *Leading for results: Transforming teaching, learning, and relationships in schools.* Thousand Oaks, CA: Corwin Press.

Stine, R. (1994). *The world of Richard Stine.* New York: Welcome Enterprises.

Telushkin, J. (1996). *Words that hurt, words that heal: How to choose words wisely and well.* New York: William Morrow.

Ury, W. (2007). *The power of a positive no: How to say no and still get to yes.* New York: Bantam.

Wellman, B., & Lipton, L. (2003). *Data-driven dialogue: A facilitator's guide to collaborative inquiry.* Sherman, CT: MiraVia.

Williamson, M. (1992). *A return to love: Reflections on the principles of a Course in Miracles.* New York: HarperCollins.

Young, S. (2007). *MicroMessaging: Why great leadership is beyond words.* Chicago: McGraw-Hill.

Index

Note: Page numbers in *italics* indicate tables and figures.

CORWIN

A SAGE Company

The Corwin logo—a raven striding across an open book—represents the union of courage and learning. Corwin is committed to improving education for all learners by publishing books and other professional development resources for those serving the field of PreK–12 education. By providing practical, hands-on materials, Corwin continues to carry out the promise of its motto: **"Helping Educators Do Their Work Better."**

CPSIA information can be obtained
at www.ICGtesting.com
Printed in the USA
BVHW061032250222
630047BV00006BA/25